The AI Explosion

How Generative Intelligence Is Reshaping Work, Power, and Everyday Life

Nathan Venture , D.

Contents

Introduction

The AI explosion did not arrive as a single invention or a single product. It arrived as a shift in what software can do. For decades, most digital tools followed instructions written by people: if this happens, do that; if the user clicks here, show that. Generative systems are different. They do not merely retrieve, sort, or classify information. They produce language, images, code, plans, summaries, and variations that look and feel like work done by a capable assistant. That change sounds subtle until it is experienced directly. Then it becomes hard to ignore.

What makes the moment feel so disruptive is not just that these systems are new, but that they are useful in ordinary settings. They can draft an email, rewrite a report, outline a presentation, translate a paragraph, suggest code, or help a student start an assignment. They are not perfect, and they are not magical. But they are flexible enough to fit into many routines at once. A tool that can help with writing, analysis, customer support, research, design, and planning is not a niche tool. It begins to look like a general-purpose capability.

That generality is what gives the current wave its force. Earlier waves of AI were often impressive in narrow domains: recognizing faces, recommending products, detecting fraud, or playing a game at superhuman levels. Those systems mattered, but they were usually embedded inside specialized workflows and hidden from most users. Generative AI is different because it meets people where work already happens: in documents, inboxes, chat windows, search bars, and creative tools. The interface is simple enough that the complexity stays in the background, while the output appears immediately in front of the user.

This is why the change often feels faster than the understanding of it. People tend to notice the result before they understand the mechanism. A manager sees a first draft produced in seconds. A teacher sees a student submit polished prose that may not reflect deep understanding. A developer sees a routine task compressed into minutes. A customer service team sees response times fall. A marketing group sees content volume rise. In each case, the immediate experience is practical, not theoretical. The implications come later.

The speed of adoption also reflects a familiar pattern in technology: when a tool reduces friction across many different tasks, it spreads through the edges of an organization before it is fully planned at the center. Employees test it privately. Teams adopt it unevenly. Leaders notice both the gains and the risks after use has already begun. That creates a sense of acceleration, because the technology is not waiting for a formal rollout to become consequential. It is entering daily habits one interaction at a time.

At the same time, the AI explosion is being driven by a deeper change in the economics of intelligence. The cost of generating text, images, and code has fallen enough that many kinds of "thinking work" can now be assisted at scale. This does not mean human expertise is disappearing. It means the threshold for getting useful support has dropped. Tasks that once required a specialist, a long turnaround, or a large budget can now be approximated quickly and cheaply. That alters expectations. Once people become used to faster drafts, faster answers, and faster iteration, the old pace starts to feel like a constraint rather than a norm.

Generative AI also matters because it blurs the line between tool and collaborator. Traditional software tends to be used as an instrument: you enter data, and it returns a result. Generative systems can participate more actively in the process. They can brainstorm, rephrase, compare options, and continue a thread of work. That creates a different relationship between user and machine. The user is no longer only operating software; the user is often steering an output-producing system that can respond in natural language and adapt to instructions on the fly.

That responsiveness is powerful, but it can also be misleading. Because the systems speak fluently, people may assume they understand more than they do. Because they produce polished output, people may mistake style for reliability. Because they are helpful in one context, people may overextend them into another. The danger is not only that they can be wrong. It is that they can be wrong in ways that look confident, coherent, and complete.

Still, dismissing the technology as a novelty would miss the larger point. The AI explosion is not just about chatbots or content generation. It is about a new layer of capability being added to digital life—one that can compress time, lower barriers, and change what individuals and institutions expect from knowledge work. As with earlier waves of computing, the first visible uses are only the beginning. The more important changes often come when the technology is absorbed into processes that were not originally designed for it.

That is why the questions around AI are not limited to whether a model is impressive. The more consequential questions are what kinds of work it can reshape, how quickly organizations will reorganize around it, who gains leverage from it, and what happens when a general-purpose capability becomes cheap enough to use everywhere. The answers to those questions are already beginning to affect how people write, learn, decide, hire, market, manage, and create.

CHAPTER 1

Chapter 1: What the AI Explosion Is—and Why It Matters Now

The shift now underway is not just another upgrade in software; it is a change in what people can ask machines to do and how quickly those machines can be woven into ordinary work. For years, digital tools were valuable because they were reliable, specialized, and predictable. The new wave is different enough to unsettle that pattern, yet familiar enough to slip into existing habits before users fully register what has changed. That is why the impact often shows up first in small moments—a draft written faster, a search replaced by a conversation, a task completed with less effort—before it becomes visible as a larger transformation.

What generative intelligence does differently from traditional software

Traditional software is built to follow rules. A programmer defines the steps, the conditions, and the expected output, and the system executes that logic the same way every time. If a user wants a report, a spreadsheet formula, a search filter, or a payroll calculation, the software performs a specific operation that was anticipated in advance. Its strength is precision. Its behavior is bounded. It does what it was told to do, not what it has inferred might be useful.

Generative intelligence works differently. Instead of waiting for a prewritten instruction for every possible case, it learns patterns from large amounts of data and uses those patterns to produce new text, images, code, audio, or other outputs. In that sense, it is less like a fixed machine and more like a system that can improvise within learned limits. Research on generative AI describes this shift as moving from discriminative systems, which classify or sort, toward systems that can create novel outputs [1]. That is the key change: the software is no longer only recognizing or retrieving. It is generating.

This difference matters because generation is more flexible than rule-following. A conventional application can only do what it has been explicitly designed to do, which makes it reliable but narrow. A generative system can respond to a prompt, a partial idea, or even a rough request and then fill in the missing pieces. It can draft an email from a few bullet points, summarize a long document, suggest a product description, rewrite a paragraph in a different tone, or produce several alternatives at once. The user is not selecting from a fixed menu of outcomes so much as steering a probabilistic process toward a useful result.

That flexibility also changes the relationship between the user and the tool. Traditional software often requires the user to know the right format, the right field, or the right sequence of commands. Generative systems lower that barrier by accepting ordinary language and incomplete instructions. A person can ask for "a more concise version," "a friendlier tone," or "three options for a presentation opening," and the system can usually produce something sensible. This is one reason the technology feels so accessible so quickly: it translates broad intent into a usable draft without requiring the user to know how the draft is assembled.

At the same time, generative intelligence is not simply a smarter version of the old kind of software. Traditional programs are deterministic: the same input produces the same output, or nearly so. Generative systems are probabilistic: they estimate what response is most likely to fit the prompt and the patterns they have learned. That is why they can be surprisingly creative and also occasionally wrong, inconsistent, or overconfident. They do not "understand" in the human sense, and they do not verify truth by default. They generate what fits the pattern, not necessarily what is factually correct.

This is why generative tools can feel both powerful and unstable. A spreadsheet formula either works or it does not. A generative model may give a polished answer that sounds right while quietly missing a constraint, inventing a detail, or choosing the wrong emphasis. The output often looks finished because the system is optimized to produce fluent language and coherent structure. But fluency is not the same as accuracy. The user still has to judge whether the answer is complete, relevant, and trustworthy.

The practical implication is that generative intelligence expands what software can do without removing the need for human direction. Traditional software excels when the task is fixed, measurable, and repetitive. Generative systems excel when the task is open-ended, language-heavy, or creative enough that a useful first draft is more valuable than a perfect final answer. In that way, the new tools do not replace every older form of software. They add a new layer of capability: one that can turn intent into content, options, and structure much faster than people could assemble them alone [13].

Why the current wave reached a tipping point now

The current wave reached a tipping point when several separate ingredients stopped improving in isolation and started reinforcing one another. Models got better at language, code, images, and reasoning-like tasks. Computing power became easier to rent on demand. The cost of experimenting fell. And, crucially, the systems became simple enough for ordinary people to try without needing a technical team in the room. That combination matters because technology adoption rarely turns on raw capability alone. It turns when usefulness becomes visible, access becomes easy, and the friction of trying something new drops below the threshold of hesitation.

For years, AI was impressive in research settings but awkward in everyday use. Early systems were narrow, brittle, and expensive to train. They could classify images, translate text, or beat humans at specific games, but they did not feel like flexible tools for general work. The recent wave changed that perception because the systems began producing outputs that looked immediately useful to nonexperts: drafts, summaries, explanations, code snippets, brainstorms, and customer-facing messages. Once people could ask for something in ordinary language and receive a plausible result within seconds, the technology stopped being a distant scientific achievement and started becoming a practical interface for work.

Another reason the tipping point came now is that the underlying economics shifted. The cost of using powerful models has been falling even as quality has improved, which makes broad deployment more realistic. A tool that is merely clever in a demo does not change much. A tool that can be used repeatedly across thousands of employees, customers, or students begins to alter workflows. Research on generative AI and business performance suggests that low-cost, scalable AI assistance can improve decision-making in open-ended tasks, though the benefits are uneven and depend on how the tool is used [14]. That unevenness is important: the breakthrough is not that AI automatically makes every task better, but that it is now cheap and accessible enough to test across many tasks at once.

The timing also reflects a feedback loop between model design and user demand. Better models attract more users. More users produce more feedback, more integration, and more pressure to improve reliability and usability. Companies then release updated systems faster, not only because they can, but because competitors are doing the same. In a market where the product is improving quickly, standing still can feel like falling behind. That creates a self-reinforcing cycle: adoption accelerates development, and development accelerates adoption. What once looked like a laboratory advance becomes a platform shift because the surrounding ecosystem starts adapting to it.

There is also a psychological threshold that matters. People do not adopt new technology only when it is perfect; they adopt it when it is good enough to save time, reduce effort, or lower the cost of a mistake. Generative systems crossed that line in many everyday contexts. They may not always be right, but they are often fast, available, and helpful enough to become the first draft of a response rather than the final one. That is a major change in behavior. Once users begin treating AI as a default starting point, the technology becomes embedded in routines before organizations have fully formalized rules around it.

This is why the current wave feels larger than a normal software upgrade. General-purpose technologies do not transform the economy by replacing one task in one industry; they spread through many sectors, changing how work is organized and how value is created. Recent economic analysis describes AI in exactly these terms: as a general-purpose technology with the capacity to influence productivity and growth across a wide range of activities [15]. That kind of technology reaches a tipping point when it stops being a specialized tool for experts and starts becoming a flexible layer that can sit inside ordinary operations.

The result is not that everything changed overnight. It is that enough things changed at once to make the change obvious. Better models, cheaper access, broader usefulness, and competitive pressure all arrived together. That convergence is what turned AI from a promising field into a visible force. The tipping point was not a single invention. It was the moment when the technology became useful enough, available enough, and adaptable enough to begin reshaping the way people work and decide almost everywhere at once.

The difference between narrow tools and general-purpose capabilities

The difference between a narrow tool and a general-purpose capability is the difference between software that solves one defined problem and software that can be pointed at many different problems with only a prompt or a few examples. A narrow tool is built for a bounded task. It may be excellent at that task, but its usefulness stops where its design stops. A general-purpose capability is broader. It does not merely automate one step in a workflow; it can be adapted across tasks, departments, and contexts, often by people who are not programmers and who may not even think of themselves as using "software" in the traditional sense.

This distinction matters because the AI boom is not only about better tools. It is about tools that behave more like flexible labor. A spreadsheet calculates. A search engine retrieves. A customer service script follows branches. Generative systems can draft, revise, summarize, translate, classify, brainstorm, and explain. The same underlying model may help write an email in the morning, outline a presentation at noon, and generate a block of code in the afternoon. That breadth is what makes the current wave feel different from earlier automation. The system is not locked to one job description.

Narrow tools still matter, and in many cases they remain the better choice. A specialized fraud detector, medical imaging model, or scheduling optimizer can outperform a general system because it is tuned to a specific environment and measured against a specific outcome. Narrow tools are usually easier to test, easier to govern, and easier to trust when the stakes are high. They are often embedded deep inside a process, where accuracy and consistency matter more than flexibility. In that sense, narrowness is not a weakness. It is a design choice that trades breadth for reliability.

General-purpose capabilities create a different kind of value because they can be reused across many workflows without being rebuilt from scratch each time. A manager can ask one system to turn meeting notes into an action list, a policy draft, and a client update. A teacher can use it to generate practice questions, simplify a reading passage, and suggest feedback on student writing. A small business owner can use it to draft marketing copy, analyze customer messages, and create a first pass at a proposal. The same capability travels across use cases, which lowers the cost of trying it in new places. That is one reason adoption can spread so quickly once people discover a useful pattern.

That flexibility also changes the structure of work. With narrow software, organizations often digitize a process by fitting people around the tool. With general-purpose AI, the tool can be fitted around the person's intent. Instead of asking whether a task can be automated end to end, leaders start asking which parts of a task can be accelerated, improved, or partially completed by a system that can understand ordinary language. This shifts attention from fixed workflows to adaptable ones. It also means the same system may affect many roles at once, not because it replaces a single job, but because it touches the writing, analysis, planning, and communication that sit inside so many jobs [3].

The breadth of these systems creates an important management challenge: the same general capability can be helpful in one context and risky in another. A model that is perfectly useful for drafting a memo may be inappropriate for making a legal judgment. A system that works well for internal brainstorming may be dangerous if it is treated as a source of truth. The more general the capability, the more carefully people must decide where to use it, where to constrain it, and where to keep humans firmly in charge. That is why adoption is not just a technical question. It is a question of boundaries.

For ordinary users, the practical effect is that AI often feels less like a single product and more like a new layer of assistance that can be attached to many products. The boundary between the tool and the task becomes blurry. People do not always notice when they have shifted from using software to delegating work to a system that is generating language, options, or decisions on their behalf. That is part of the power of general-purpose capability: it slips into existing habits. It does not always announce itself as a dramatic transformation. Often it appears as a small convenience that is useful enough to repeat, then flexible enough to spread.

As organizations experiment more deeply, they also encounter the limits of generality. A broad system may be impressive in a demo and uneven in a real workflow. It may need human review, better instructions, or tighter guardrails. It may perform well at generating possibilities but poorly at choosing among them. It may be fast without being dependable. These tradeoffs are not signs that the technology is failing; they are signs that breadth comes with ambiguity. The more a system can do, the more important it becomes to define what it should not do, and the more valuable human judgment becomes in deciding when a narrow tool is still the right one.

Why everyday users feel the change before they fully understand it

The change usually registers first as convenience, not transformation. A person asks a chatbot to draft an email, summarize a meeting, rewrite a paragraph, or generate a list of ideas, and the result arrives fast enough to feel almost casual. The user does not need to learn a new workflow or wait for a formal rollout. The tool simply appears inside the habits already in place. That is one reason the shift can feel larger than it looks on paper: it enters through ordinary tasks that people already know how to do, then quietly lowers the effort required to do them again and again. That pattern is especially powerful because many of the first benefits are visible before the deeper mechanics are understood. A manager may notice that a report gets drafted in minutes instead of hours. A student may see a rough outline appear before they have organized their thoughts. A customer service representative may use a generative assistant to rephrase a difficult response. None of those moments require the user to understand training data, model architecture, or prompt design. The system feels useful because it produces a plausible starting point, and in many settings a good starting point is already a major advantage. This is consistent with broader research on generative AI, which emphasizes its ability to produce novel outputs rather than merely classify or retrieve information [1].

People also feel the change before they understand it because the outputs resemble human work closely enough to be immediately legible. Traditional software often announces itself as software: a form, a filter, a dashboard, a menu. Generative systems blur that boundary. They speak in natural language, imitate familiar formats, and can adapt to the tone or structure a user asks for. That makes the interaction feel less like operating a machine and more like delegating to a junior collaborator. The result is psychologically significant. Users do not experience the tool as a specialized instrument sitting at the edge of their workflow; they experience it as something that can stand in the middle of the workflow and help carry the load.

At the same time, the speed of adoption is shaped by a simple fact about human behavior: people are quicker to notice time saved than system changes. If a tool helps you finish a task before lunch, you remember the convenience immediately. If the same tool changes how drafts are evaluated, how assignments are written, how customer expectations are set, or how teams divide labor, those effects emerge more slowly. They accumulate across repeated use. The first impression is often that the tool is merely assisting. Only later does it become clear that the surrounding process has begun to reorganize around what the tool can do well.

This is why the AI boom often spreads through small, unofficial experiments before it becomes a formal policy issue. Individuals try it on their own. Teams notice that some people are using it to move faster. Managers see uneven but real gains. Then organizations begin asking where the tool belongs, what it should be used for, and what risks it creates. In other words, understanding usually lags behind adoption. The practical question comes first: Can this help me now? The analytical question comes later: What kind of system is this, and what does it change in the long run?

There is also a deeper reason the change feels hard to pin down. Generative systems do not replace a single well-defined machine function; they alter the boundary between thinking, drafting, searching, and editing. Those boundaries are familiar in human work, but they are not always visible in software. When a tool can help with many adjacent tasks, it becomes easier to absorb into existing routines and harder to label as a distinct category. That broad usefulness is part of what makes generative intelligence so disruptive. It does not announce itself as a revolution in the abstract. It arrives as a set of small capabilities that fit into familiar work, then gradually make some of that work faster, cheaper, and more elastic.

For everyday users, that means the first encounter is often not awe but relief. The machine is not replacing every judgment call or solving every problem. It is removing friction from the first draft, the first search, the first explanation, the first version. That is enough to change behavior. Once a person has experienced a tool that can turn a blank page into something workable, or a rough idea into something usable, the threshold for what feels possible shifts. The change is felt before it is fully understood because the experience is immediate, personal, and practical long before it becomes conceptual.

CHAPTER 2

Chapter 2: The Hidden Engines Behind the Boom

What looks like a sudden leap in capability is usually the result of several quieter forces gathering strength at once. The visible product may be a chatbot, an image generator, or a coding assistant, but behind it are choices about what data the system learns from, how much computing power can be brought to bear, and how the model itself is designed to turn patterns into useful output. Those ingredients do not operate in isolation. They reinforce one another, and when they do, the results can surprise even the people building the systems.

Data, compute, and model design as the core ingredients

The first ingredient is data, but not in the vague sense of "lots of information." What matters is the kind of data, how it is cleaned, how it is labeled, and how well it reflects the task the model is meant to do. A language model trained on broad internet text will absorb patterns of grammar, style, facts, opinions, and mistakes all at once. A model trained on code learns different regularities. A model trained on medical records, product catalogs, or customer conversations learns still other patterns. In every case, the model is not memorizing the world as it is; it is learning from the traces the world leaves behind. That means the quality of the input matters as much as the quantity. Messy, biased, outdated, or narrow data can produce a system that is fluent but unreliable, confident but incomplete.

This is one reason the AI boom has accelerated so quickly. Organizations and researchers have spent years collecting digital exhaust: documents, images, logs, transcripts, clicks, purchases, code, and sensor readings. Much of that material was created for other purposes, not for AI, which makes it especially valuable. Once a system can learn from that accumulated record at scale, it can extract patterns that would be impossible for a human team to notice manually. In some domains, the data itself becomes the moat. Whoever has access to richer, more relevant, or more proprietary data can often build a stronger system, or at least a system that is more useful in a specific setting. That is why companies in healthcare, finance, manufacturing, and retail care so much about their internal data, even when the public conversation focuses mostly on flashy chatbots.

The second ingredient is compute, which is shorthand for the enormous amount of processing power needed to train and run these models. Training a large model is not like installing ordinary software. It can require clusters of specialized chips working for days, weeks, or longer, with electricity, cooling, networking, and orchestration all built around the effort. The more compute available, the larger and more complex the model can be, and the more experiments a team can run while trying to improve it. This matters because model development is partly an engineering problem and partly a search problem: researchers test architectures, adjust training methods, compare outputs, and repeat the process many times. Greater compute does not guarantee a breakthrough, but it expands the range of what can be tried and the speed at which progress can compound.

Compute also affects who can participate. When training costs were low enough for small teams, experimentation was cheap and fragmented. As models grew more capable, the price of competing rose sharply. That pushed the frontier toward large labs, major technology firms, and well-funded startups that could afford the chips and infrastructure. At the same time, the cost of using these models has been falling, which is why end users can now access capabilities that once required specialized research environments. The result is a split between the expensive process of building frontier systems and the increasingly accessible process of deploying them. That split helps explain why the technology can feel both centralized and widely available at the same time.

The third ingredient is model design, and this is where the raw materials become something useful. A model architecture determines how the system represents patterns, how it processes sequences, how it balances memory and flexibility, and how it turns training into prediction. Small design choices can have large consequences. A model may be better at long context, more stable in training, more efficient to run, or more responsive to human feedback. In practice, the breakthrough often comes not from one dramatic invention but from the combination of architecture, training objective, optimization method, and post-training refinement. Generative AI is a good example of how innovation often works by combining existing techniques in a new way rather than inventing everything from scratch [13].

That combination is what makes the systems feel unexpectedly capable. A model trained on broad data with enough compute and a well-chosen design can begin to generalize across tasks it was never explicitly programmed to perform. It can draft a memo after seeing examples of good business writing, summarize a document it has never encountered before, or produce code that resembles patterns it has learned from millions of prior snippets. This is not magic and not understanding in the human sense. It is pattern learning at a scale that allows useful abstraction. The system does not need to know what a meeting is the way a person does; it only needs to learn enough about the structure of meeting notes, agendas, and action items to produce something that fits the pattern.

Because these ingredients reinforce one another, gains can arrive in jumps rather than in smooth increments. Better data can make a model more useful. More compute can make it possible to train on that data more effectively. Better design can let the system extract more value from both. And once a model becomes useful enough, more people use it, which creates more feedback, more fine-tuning opportunities, and more pressure to improve it further. That is why the AI boom has the feel of a flywheel. The visible product may be a polished interface, but the real engine is the interaction among information, processing power, and architecture. When those three align, capability can advance faster than intuition expects.

How scale creates surprising new capabilities

One of the most important features of generative AI is that its abilities do not grow in a straight line. They often appear to change qualitatively once the system reaches a larger scale. A model trained on more data, with more computing power, and with a better design can seem not just a little better, but different in kind. It may begin to follow longer instructions, sustain a more coherent style, handle a wider range of topics, or combine pieces of information in ways that were not obvious in smaller versions. That is why people sometimes describe these systems as if they have crossed a threshold. The underlying reason is not mystery; it is that scale can unlock patterns and relationships that smaller models never had enough capacity to represent reliably.

This matters because many of the skills people care about are not isolated skills. Writing a useful email is not one thing; it involves tone, purpose, audience, structure, concision, and often a degree of persuasion. Summarizing a meeting is not just compressing text; it is deciding what matters, what can be left out, and how to preserve the main thread. At small scale, a model may do one of these tasks adequately and fail at the rest. At larger scale, it may begin to coordinate them. The result is not perfect understanding, but a broader and more flexible response. In practice, that flexibility is what makes the system feel suddenly more capable than older software, even when the user has not changed the prompt much at all.

Scale also changes the range of contexts a model can handle. A system with limited capacity may work well only when the task is narrow and the wording is familiar. Increase the scale, and the same type of system can often tolerate ambiguity, infer intent from incomplete instructions, and adapt to different writing styles or domains. It may be able to draft in a formal voice one moment and a conversational voice the next, or move from brainstorming to editing to translation without being retrained for each step. This is one reason generative AI is so often described as general-purpose. The model is not merely solving a single problem more efficiently; it is becoming more reusable across problems, which is a very different kind of value.

Another surprising effect of scale is that new abilities can emerge at the edges before they are obvious in the center. A smaller model may be noticeably weaker on math, logic, code, or multi-step reasoning. A larger model may not become a mathematician or a programmer in the human sense, but it can improve enough to be useful in partial ways: suggesting a function, spotting an error, explaining a concept, or helping a user work through a first draft. These are not trivial gains. In many real workflows, partial competence is enough to save time, reduce friction, or lower the barrier to starting. That is why the practical impact of scale often shows up first in assistance rather than automation. The system does not need to replace the expert to become valuable; it only needs to make the expert faster or more effective.

There is also a compounding effect. Better models attract more users, more feedback, more investment, and more pressure to improve the surrounding product. Better products make the model easier to use, which increases adoption. More adoption creates more opportunities to observe where the system helps and where it fails. That feedback loop does not guarantee progress, but it makes progress faster once the system has crossed a certain level of usefulness. In other words, scale is not only about the size of the model itself. It is also about the ecosystem that forms around it: the tools, interfaces, workflows, and business incentives that make the model more accessible and more embedded in daily work.

This is why large-scale generative systems can feel so different from earlier AI tools. Traditional software often improved by becoming more precise within a fixed task. Scaled generative systems can improve by becoming more adaptable across many tasks at once. That broader adaptability is what lets them enter ordinary work so quickly. A tool that can draft, revise, explain, translate, and brainstorm is not just a better version of a narrow application; it begins to sit in the middle of knowledge work itself. Research on generative AI has emphasized this shift from narrowly discriminative tasks toward more creative and open-ended production [1].

But scale should not be confused with reliability. A larger model can be more capable and still be wrong in confident, costly, or hard-to-detect ways. In fact, greater fluency can make errors more persuasive. That is part of what makes scale so consequential: it raises the ceiling on useful performance while also making the output feel more trustworthy than it always is. For organizations and individuals, the lesson is not that bigger models are magically better in every situation. It is that scale can create a new class of capability—broad, flexible, and fast enough to matter in everyday work—while still requiring human judgment to decide when the result is ready to use and when it needs checking.

The business incentives pushing rapid release and adoption

The pressure to release quickly is built into the business model itself. In the old software world, companies often competed by polishing a product before launch, charging for access, and then improving it in measured updates. With generative AI, the product improves not only through engineering, but through use. Every new user can reveal weaknesses, surface new demand, and create data that helps the system get better. That changes the incentives. A company that waits too long risks losing mindshare, developer loyalty, enterprise contracts, and the chance to become the default interface people reach for first.

There is also a simple market logic at work: the first system that feels broadly useful can attract an outsized share of attention, even if later versions are better. In fast-moving categories, being "good enough" early can matter more than being perfect later. That is especially true when the product is easy to try, easy to share, and easy to slot into existing workflows. A chatbot, writing assistant, or coding tool can spread through teams by informal adoption long before a formal procurement process finishes. Once that happens, the company behind it gains not just users, but habits, data, and a stronger position in the next round of competition.

This is one reason business-model innovation has become as important as model innovation. Generative AI is not only a technical breakthrough; it is a new way to package capabilities, price access, and build recurring relationships with users [4]. Some firms sell subscriptions to individuals. Others bundle AI into enterprise platforms. Others offer application programming interfaces so outside developers can build on top of their models. In each case, rapid release serves a strategic purpose: it helps establish the product as infrastructure before competitors can define the standard. The company that becomes the default layer for writing, searching, coding, or customer support may control a valuable gateway to future revenue.

Speed is also encouraged by the economics of expectation. Investors, customers, and partners often reward visible momentum more than invisible refinement. A company that announces new capabilities, expands access, and shows rapid iteration can appear to be leading the market, even if the underlying system is still uneven. That creates a pressure cycle. Leadership wants growth. Growth requires adoption. Adoption requires visibility. Visibility requires frequent releases. The result is a race to keep shipping, testing, and repositioning the product in public, sometimes before the organization has fully solved the operational or safety questions that come with wider use.

Enterprise buyers add another layer of incentive. Large organizations are not simply purchasing software; they are trying to reduce labor costs, speed up output, and keep pace with competitors. If a tool can draft documents, summarize meetings, assist with code, or support customer service, the savings can be immediate enough to justify experimentation. That makes adoption easier to sell internally, especially when the alternative is waiting for a more mature version that might arrive after rivals have already gained efficiency. Research on AI adoption in production settings consistently points to organizational readiness, perceived usefulness, and strategic fit as major drivers of uptake [30]. In practice, that means vendors are rewarded for making the tool easy to pilot, easy to integrate, and easy to demonstrate in a business case.

The same forces also explain why companies often release imperfect systems and then improve them in public. A model does not have to be flawless to be commercially valuable; it has to be useful enough to create a habit. Once users depend on it, the company has time to harden the product, refine safeguards, and expand into adjacent tasks. That approach can be rational from a business standpoint, but it also shifts risk outward. Users become part of the testing environment. Managers become responsible for deciding where the tool is reliable enough, where it needs human review, and where the cost of error is too high. The market rewards rapid adoption, but the burden of judgment does not disappear. It moves downstream.

That is why the push for speed is not just about ambition or hype. It reflects a deeper competition over distribution, data, and default behavior. The company that gets into a workflow first can learn from real usage, improve faster, and make it harder for others to displace it. The company that waits may produce a safer or more elegant system, but still find itself chasing a market already organized around someone else's interface. In generative AI, release timing is not a minor operational detail. It is part of the strategy.

Why competition is speeding up the pace of change

Competition is one of the strongest accelerants in the AI market because no major player can afford to stand still. Once one company demonstrates a useful new capability—better writing, faster coding, stronger search, more natural conversation, or a feature that saves users time—rivals are forced to respond. They do not need to believe the first mover has solved the problem perfectly. They only need to believe that customers will notice a gap. In a crowded market, even a small advantage can become a reason to switch, experiment, or renegotiate which tools a team uses.

That pressure is intensified by the fact that generative AI is not just a product category; it is becoming a layer inside many product categories. Search engines, office suites, customer service platforms, design tools, development environments, analytics systems, and education software are all being reshaped by the same underlying capability. When AI becomes a feature rather than a standalone app, competition spreads across the entire software landscape. A company is no longer competing only with direct rivals. It is competing with the expectation that its product should now be smarter, faster, and easier to use than before. That expectation can move quickly from novelty to baseline.

The result is a race on multiple fronts at once. Companies compete on model quality, but also on price, speed, reliability, context length, multimodal abilities, and how easily the system fits into existing workflows. They compete on distribution, because the best model is less valuable if users cannot reach it easily. They compete on developer ecosystems, because third-party tools and integrations can make one platform stickier than another. And they compete on brand trust, because users increasingly want to know whether a system is safe, stable, and worth depending on for real work. This is why the pace of change can feel frantic: each improvement by one player forces others to move in several directions at once.

There is also a structural reason the cycle speeds up. In many software markets, the product improves as it is used, which means adoption itself becomes part of the competitive engine. More users create more feedback, more visibility into failures, and more pressure to refine the system. That makes the launch strategy different from older technology markets, where companies could wait until a product felt finished. Here, the market often rewards early release, rapid iteration, and public learning. A company that hesitates risks not only losing customers but also losing the chance to shape user habits, developer loyalty, and the standards around which the market organizes itself. Research on AI as a general-purpose technology emphasizes that its effects can spill across the economy through innovation, productivity, and self-reinforcing improvement [15].

Competition also compresses time because the cost of waiting is not just lost revenue; it is strategic irrelevance. If a competitor trains users to expect instant summaries, automated drafting, or AI-assisted analysis, then every slower product begins to look old-fashioned even if it still works well. That is especially true in business settings, where managers compare tools not only by technical performance but by how much labor they save and how quickly they can be deployed. Once one vendor shows that a workflow can be shortened, rivals are under pressure to match or exceed it—or explain why their slower approach is somehow better. In practice, that often means shipping sooner, revising more often, and accepting a degree of roughness that would have been unacceptable in earlier eras.

The feedback loop reaches beyond product teams into the broader economy. As firms adopt AI to move faster, their competitors must do the same simply to keep up. A company that uses AI to draft proposals faster, respond to customers sooner, or prototype ideas more cheaply can gain a short-term edge. But that edge does not stay private for long. Others imitate the workflow, buy similar tools, or build their own. What begins as an advantage for one firm becomes an industry-wide expectation. Over time, the competition shifts from “Should we use AI?” to “How much faster can we use it than everyone else?” That shift is one reason the technology spreads even in organizations that are cautious by nature.

This dynamic can be healthy, but it can also be destabilizing. When the market rewards speed above all else, companies may release systems before they are fully reliable, or adopt them before they have clear rules for oversight. That does not happen because leaders are careless so much as because the competitive environment narrows their options. If rivals are moving, standing still feels risky. The pressure to match the pace can push organizations into a posture of constant experimentation, where the cost of delay seems larger than the cost of uncertainty. At the same time, users benefit from a rapid flow of improvements, lower prices, and more capable tools. The tension is built into the structure of the race: competition makes the technology better faster, but it also makes the environment harder to govern cleanly.

CHAPTER 3

Chapter 3: How Generative AI Actually Works for Non-Experts

To understand generative AI clearly, it helps to separate the machinery from the experience of using it. On the surface, these systems feel conversational and immediate, as if a knowledgeable assistant were sitting on the other side of the screen. Underneath, they are built from patterns learned during training and from the way they turn a prompt into a likely next output, one step at a time. That gap between appearance and mechanism is where many of the most important misunderstandings begin. It is also where the practical questions live: why the system can be so useful, why it can fail in ways that seem strange, and why a polished answer is not the same thing as a verified one.

A simple explanation of training, prompting, and output generation

Training is the part most people never see, but it is where the system acquires its general habits. Before a model can answer a question or draft a paragraph, it is exposed to huge collections of examples—text, code, images, or other data—and adjusted so that it becomes better at recognizing patterns in them. The goal is not to store every example like a filing cabinet. It is to learn statistical relationships: which words tend to appear together, how sentences usually unfold, how code structures are formed, how one idea follows another. In that sense, training is less like programming a fixed procedure and more like shaping a very large pattern-recognition engine. Research on generative AI describes this shift as moving from narrow, discriminative systems toward models that can produce novel outputs across tasks [1].

That training process is why these systems can seem so flexible. A model that has learned from enough varied material is not limited to one job. It can draft, summarize, translate, classify, brainstorm, and imitate tone because those abilities are all related to the patterns it has absorbed. But training is also why the system can be impressively fluent without being grounded in the way a person is grounded. It does not "know" facts in the human sense. It has learned associations among tokens, not lived experience, and not a built-in sense of truth. The model's internal strength is pattern completion. Its weakness is that pattern completion can continue even when the pattern is wrong, incomplete, or misleading.

Prompting is the part the user sees. A prompt is the instruction, question, example, or context you provide to steer the model toward a desired result. It can be as short as "write a polite follow-up email" or as detailed as a multi-paragraph brief with audience, tone, constraints, and examples. In practice, prompting is not magic language. It is a way of narrowing the model's broad capabilities toward a specific task. The more clearly the prompt defines the goal, the format, and the boundaries, the more likely the output will be useful. But even a good prompt does not force certainty. It simply gives the model a better starting point for generating a plausible response.

This is one reason people often underestimate how much of the work is done by framing. A model asked for "ideas" will behave differently from one asked for "three options ranked by risk," or "a draft for a skeptical executive audience," or "a checklist with no more than seven items." The prompt changes the shape of the response because it changes what the model treats as most likely to come next. In business settings, that makes prompting less like issuing a command and more like conducting a conversation with a highly capable but literal collaborator. The quality of the exchange depends on clarity, context, and iteration. Studies of organizational use show that human and generative AI can complement each other in decision-making when the interaction is structured well [49].

Output generation is the final step, and it is where the system's actual method becomes easiest to misunderstand. The model does not retrieve a finished answer from a database. It generates one piece at a time, predicting the next token, then the next, then the next, based on the prompt and everything it has produced so far. That step-by-step process is what gives the output its smoothness. It is also why the result can drift. If the early part of the response takes a wrong turn, the later part may continue confidently down the same path. The system is not checking its own work the way a careful human editor might. It is extending a sequence in the direction that seems most probable.

That probabilistic character explains both the power and the fragility of generative AI. Because it is generating rather than retrieving, it can produce fresh wording, alternative phrasings, and combinations that were never explicitly stored. That is what makes it useful for drafting, ideation, coding support, and many forms of synthesis. But the same mechanism can produce errors that sound polished. A model may supply a convincing answer that is partly right, partly invented, or simply mismatched to the question. The surface form of confidence does not guarantee the substance of accuracy. This is one reason generative AI has spread so quickly across more than 350 documented applications while still requiring careful human oversight in many settings [48].

The practical implication is that training, prompting, and output generation are three different stages of one workflow, and each stage has its own limits. Training gives the model its broad capability. Prompting directs that capability toward a task. Output generation turns the result into language, code, or another form people can use. When a system succeeds, it can feel almost effortless because all three stages are hidden behind a simple interface. When it fails, the failure may appear inexplicable unless you remember that the model is not reasoning from first principles or verifying every claim. It is producing the most likely continuation given what it has learned and what the prompt has asked for.

That is why the most effective users do not treat the model as an oracle. They treat it as a tool that responds to framing. They ask for drafts, alternatives, summaries, and structured comparisons. They check important outputs against other sources. They revise prompts when the result is too vague, too narrow, or too confident. In other words, they use the system as part of a process rather than as the final authority. Once that distinction is clear, the mechanics become less mysterious: training gives the model its range, prompting gives it direction, and output generation gives it form.

What these systems are good at—and where they break down

Generative systems are strongest when the task is about pattern, variation, and language-like structure. They can draft, summarize, translate, rephrase, brainstorm, classify, and combine information quickly. They are especially useful when the goal is not a single perfect answer but a good first pass, a range of options, or a compressed version of something large and messy. That is why they fit so naturally into writing, customer support, marketing, research support, coding assistance, and many forms of internal knowledge work. In those settings, they can reduce the time it takes to get from a blank page to something workable.

Their speed is part of their appeal, but it is also what makes them seem more capable than they are. A generative model does not "understand" in the human sense. It has learned statistical relationships so well that it can often produce output that looks informed, fluent, and context-aware. When the prompt is clear and the domain is familiar, the result can be impressively useful. It can mirror tone, follow instructions, and adapt to audience. It can take a rough idea and turn it into a memo, a product description, a lesson plan, or a code snippet with little friction. In many everyday situations, that is enough to save time and unlock momentum.

But the same design that makes these systems flexible also makes them vulnerable to failure. They are not grounded in reality by default. They do not verify facts unless they are connected to a separate checking mechanism, and they do not possess a built-in sense of truth. If the prompt is ambiguous, incomplete, or misleading, they may produce an answer that sounds plausible while quietly drifting away from what is correct. This is why they can be so persuasive even when they are wrong.

Fluency is not the same thing as accuracy, and confidence is not the same thing as evidence.

The breakdowns often show up in predictable places. One is specificity. The more a request depends on exact details, current information, or local context, the more likely the model is to stumble. Another is multi-step reasoning. These systems can sometimes handle chains of thought-like tasks, but they are less reliable when the task requires sustained consistency across many steps, hidden assumptions, or careful tradeoffs. They may lose track of earlier constraints, contradict themselves, or optimize for the most likely-sounding answer rather than the most defensible one. In creative work, they can generate useful material, but they can also drift toward blandness if the user does not push them toward a distinctive point of view.

They also struggle with what humans often take for granted: common sense grounded in lived experience. A model may know a great deal about the world in a statistical sense and still miss what a person would immediately notice about a situation, such as a contradiction in a document, a social nuance in an email, or the practical constraints of a workplace. It can imitate judgment, but it does not possess judgment as a stable inner capacity. That gap matters most when the output will influence a decision, a relationship, a diagnosis, a legal interpretation, or any other setting where mistakes carry consequences.

Another limit is that these systems can be too eager to fill in gaps. If they do not know something, they may not always say so plainly. Instead, they may guess. This tendency is one reason hallucinations—confident but false outputs—remain such a persistent concern. Research across AI applications has repeatedly shown that these systems can support productivity and creativity while also introducing error, bias, and misuse risk [51]. The problem is not simply that they fail; it is that they often fail in a way that is polished enough to escape casual notice.

That creates an important practical distinction. Generative AI is often excellent at producing candidate outputs, but much less dependable as a final authority. It can propose language, structure, and alternatives at high speed. It can widen the search space and make a person faster. What it cannot do reliably on its own is guarantee correctness, weigh accountability, or replace the kind of judgment that comes from experience, incentives, and responsibility. In other words, these systems are powerful accelerators of work, but they are not self-validating systems. They need boundaries, review, and context, especially as the stakes rise.

Why confidence can hide uncertainty or error

A confident answer can sound more reliable than a careful one, which is one reason generative systems can mislead users even when they appear polished. These models are built to produce the most likely continuation of a prompt, not to pause and verify every claim against reality. That means they can generate fluent explanations, tidy summaries, and decisive-sounding recommendations even when the underlying information is incomplete, outdated, or simply wrong. The output may read as if it came from a person who knows exactly what they are talking about, but the appearance of certainty is not the same thing as certainty itself.

This matters because humans are naturally inclined to trust fluency. When a response is grammatically clean, well organized, and delivered without hesitation, it can trigger the assumption that the system has done deeper reasoning than it actually has. In practice, the model may be drawing on patterns in its training data rather than on a grounded understanding of the specific question. It can sound especially convincing when the topic is familiar enough to be plausible but not familiar enough for the user to notice small errors. A wrong date, a misquoted policy, a fabricated citation, or a subtly distorted explanation can pass under the radar because the overall tone feels authoritative.

The problem is not limited to outright mistakes. Sometimes the system is uncertain in ways that are hard to detect because it does not naturally signal doubt the way a careful human would. A person might say, “I’m not sure,” or “I may be missing something,” but a model can continue producing a smooth answer even when the prompt is ambiguous or the evidence is thin. That creates a dangerous mismatch: the user sees confidence, while the system may be operating with weak support. In high-stakes settings, that mismatch can lead to bad decisions, especially when the output is treated as a finished product instead of a draft to be checked.

Researchers studying human-AI collaboration have emphasized that the value of these systems depends on how well human judgment and machine output are combined, not on blind trust in either one alone [53]. That point is especially important here. A generative model can be very useful as a first-pass thinker, but it does not automatically know when it is stretching beyond its reliable range. It may answer a question about law, medicine, finance, or policy with the same stylistic confidence it uses for a casual writing task. The surface quality stays high even as the risk of error rises.

Another reason confidence hides uncertainty is that these systems are often optimized for usefulness and user satisfaction, not for visible hesitation. If a model constantly interrupted itself with caveats, it would feel less helpful. But if it never expressed caution, it could become misleading. The result is a tension built into the experience: the system is designed to sound smooth enough to be usable, yet that smoothness can blur the line between a strong answer and a plausible guess. In effect, the model is often presenting a probability distribution as prose. The prose sounds settled even when the underlying probabilities are not.

This is why the safest way to use generative AI is to treat confidence as a clue, not proof. A polished answer may be a useful starting point, a helpful draft, or a strong suggestion, but it still needs context, verification, and judgment. The reader should pay attention not only to what the system says, but also to what it may be assuming, omitting, or compressing. A good rule is to become more cautious, not less, when the answer sounds especially smooth. The cleaner the language, the more important it becomes to ask: Is this well supported, or merely well phrased?

That habit of skepticism is not anti-AI; it is what makes AI use sustainable. Generative tools are most valuable when they accelerate thought without replacing the responsibility to check it. In that sense, confidence is useful only when it is paired with discipline. The system can draft, suggest, and organize, but the human still has to decide whether the answer is true, relevant, and safe to act on.

How to think about AI as a collaborator, not an oracle

The easiest mistake to make with generative AI is to treat it like a machine that either knows the answer or does not. That framing invites the wrong kind of trust. A better model is to think of AI as a collaborator with strengths, blind spots, and a tendency to sound more certain than it is. It can contribute draft language, surface possibilities, compress large amounts of material, and take on repetitive parts of a task. But it does not possess understanding in the human sense, and it does not carry responsibility for the result. The person using it still has to decide what matters, what is plausible, what is missing, and what should be done next.

This is why the most useful way to work with AI is not to ask, “Is it right?” as if the system were a final authority. The better question is, “What role is it playing in this task?” Sometimes it is a brainstorm partner, producing options that are meant to be evaluated, not accepted. Sometimes it is a drafting assistant, turning rough notes into a cleaner first pass. Sometimes it is a research aide, helping organize material before a human checks the sources. In each case, the value comes from speed, variation, and structure—not from unconditional truth. People who get the most from these tools usually keep the boundary clear: the model proposes, the human disposes.

That boundary matters because AI output often has the texture of competence even when the content is shaky. A response can be fluent, neatly organized, and full of confident transitions while still containing subtle errors, omissions, or invented details. This is one reason users can be lulled into overtrust. The system is optimized to generate a likely and useful continuation, not to stop and certify every statement against reality. In practical terms, that means the appearance of polish should never be mistaken for verification. A well-written answer can still be a weak answer if the underlying facts are wrong or if the framing misses the actual problem.

Working with AI as a collaborator also means giving it the right kind of assignment. Humans often get better results when they break a task into stages: ask for an outline first, then a draft, then revisions, then a check for gaps or inconsistencies. They can also ask the model to play a specific role, such as skeptic, editor, comparator, or explainer. This kind of prompting turns the system into a flexible work partner rather than a black box delivering a single verdict. It also makes the human's thinking more visible. When you ask for alternatives, objections, or assumptions, you are not just improving the output; you are exposing the structure of your own judgment.

That approach fits what research on technology adoption has long suggested: people are more likely to use new systems effectively when the tools support existing goals and workflows instead of forcing a complete mental reset. In one study of university students, perceived usefulness and ease of use were closely tied to acceptance of AI tools

[58]. That pattern is not surprising. People do not adopt a collaborator because it is impressive in the abstract. They adopt it because it makes a familiar task faster, clearer, or less burdensome. The same logic applies in professional settings. The best AI use cases are usually the ones where the system removes friction without removing human accountability.

At the same time, collaboration with AI requires a different posture toward uncertainty. In ordinary teamwork, a colleague can explain how they reached a conclusion, point to a source, or admit they are unsure. An AI system may not do any of those things reliably unless the user asks for them and then checks the result. So the user has to become the manager of the collaboration: requesting sources, comparing versions, testing edge cases, and knowing when to stop relying on the model's wording. That is especially important in work that affects money, health, legal exposure, reputation, or safety. In those settings, AI can accelerate preparation, but it should not be allowed to substitute for review.

The most productive mindset is neither awe nor suspicion. Awe leads people to outsource too much. Suspicion leads them to ignore a tool that could genuinely help. Collaboration sits in the middle. It treats AI as something like a fast, tireless junior partner: useful for generating drafts, exploring options, and handling first passes, but always in need of direction and supervision. That framing preserves the real advantage of the technology while keeping human judgment where it belongs. The system can widen the range of what one person can do, but it does not replace the person who has to decide what good work looks like.

CHAPTER 4

Chapter 4: Work Rewritten—Tasks, Jobs, and Careers in Transition

Once AI moves from a novelty to a routine part of the workday, the central question is no longer whether it can produce something useful, but where it fits inside the flow of labor. That shift forces a more precise view of work itself. Most jobs are not single activities; they are bundles of tasks, some repetitive, some judgment-heavy, some relational, and some tied to responsibility or trust. Generative systems tend to enter first through the parts of a job that are easiest to standardize, easiest to review, and easiest to hand off without changing the whole role at once.

Which tasks AI can automate first

The first tasks AI automates are usually the ones that sit closest to language, repetition, and pattern. That is not because those tasks are trivial, but because they are structurally friendly to systems that learn from examples and generate likely continuations. If a job involves drafting a standard email, summarizing a document, sorting requests into categories, rewriting text for a different audience, or extracting key fields from a form, generative AI can often produce a useful first pass quickly. These are the kinds of tasks where the output can be checked, edited, or accepted with relatively low risk. They are also the kinds of tasks that have accumulated in nearly every office, making them an obvious place for automation to begin.

In practice, the earliest gains usually come from work that is high-volume, moderately repetitive, and easy to evaluate. Customer support is a clear example. A system can draft responses to common questions, suggest replies for agents, or route a message to the right category before a human ever sees it. Marketing teams use similar tools to generate campaign variations, product descriptions, and subject lines. Administrative staff use them to turn messy notes into clean summaries, meeting follow-ups, or formatted reports. None of these tasks requires the AI to understand the entire business in a deep human sense. It only needs to handle a narrow slice of the workflow well enough to save time and reduce friction.

Language-based work is especially exposed because so much of it is already standardized. Many organizations run on templates, recurring messages, and familiar formats that have been repeated for years. AI is good at filling in those structures. It can adapt a paragraph for a new tone, turn bullet points into prose, condense a long thread into a digest, or transform one version of a document into another. That is one reason generative AI has spread so quickly through writing-heavy roles: it does not need a new business process to become useful. It can slide into the process that already exists and take over the portions that are predictable enough to delegate.

Another early target is work that involves searching, sorting, and first-draft synthesis. People often spend large amounts of time not creating something from scratch but locating information, comparing options, and assembling pieces into a coherent whole. AI can accelerate that stage by scanning text, pulling out themes, generating outlines, or suggesting next steps. In research support, legal review, sales operations, and internal knowledge management, the value is often less about replacing final judgment than about cutting down the time needed to get to a workable starting point. A task that once took an hour of reading and note-taking may shrink to a few minutes of review and correction.

Tasks become easier to automate when the cost of a mistake is limited and the output can be supervised. This is why AI reaches first into the front end of work rather than the final decision. Drafting is easier than approving. Summarizing is easier than certifying. Categorizing is easier than adjudicating. A model can help prepare a document, but a person still signs it. It can recommend a response, but a person still chooses whether to send it. It can flag anomalies, but a person still decides whether they matter. In many organizations, that division will remain important for a long time because it lets companies capture speed without surrendering accountability.

By contrast, tasks that depend on physical presence, tacit knowledge, or nuanced human trust are slower to automate. So are tasks where the environment changes constantly and the acceptable answer depends on judgment that is hard to formalize. A receptionist can be supported by AI, but a bedside nurse, a skilled tradesperson, or a manager handling conflict in a team cannot be reduced so easily to text generation. Even in white-collar settings, the most resistant tasks are often the ones that require negotiation, persuasion, leadership, or responsibility for outcomes that cannot be neatly checked by a machine. Those tasks may be assisted, but they are not first in line for full automation.

This is why the first wave of automation often looks less like job elimination than task reshaping. Generative AI tends to remove the dull center of a workflow before it touches the judgment at the edges. It takes on the repetitive drafting, the routine variation, the initial sorting, and the low-stakes explanation. What remains for people is often the part that is hardest to standardize: deciding what matters, checking for errors, handling exceptions, and making the work fit a real-world context.

Research on organizations suggests that as AI becomes embedded in daily work, its effects are felt most clearly at the level of tasks and job design, not just at the level of headline job titles [3].

That pattern matters because task automation changes power inside jobs before it changes the job itself. The person who can use AI well may produce more in less time, but they may also become responsible for a larger volume of output, a faster pace, and a thinner margin for error. The work does not disappear so much as move. Some parts become cheaper, faster, and more abundant; other parts become more valuable because they are the remaining source of judgment and trust. The first tasks AI automates are therefore not only the easiest ones. They are the ones that reveal where human effort is still essential, and where it is becoming increasingly expensive to spend time manually.

How AI changes productivity, quality, and speed

AI changes productivity first by changing the shape of work. In many jobs, the slow part is not the final decision or the final deliverable; it is the accumulation of small steps around it. Someone has to draft, revise, search, compare, summarize, format, and reformat before the real judgment call is made. Generative AI compresses those middle steps. It can produce a passable first draft in seconds, turn a long document into a short briefing, or convert rough notes into something organized enough for review. That does not eliminate the need for a human, but it changes how much time the human spends on creation versus correction.

This is why the productivity effect is often uneven. A task that once took an hour may now take ten minutes, while another task barely changes at all. The biggest gains usually appear where the work is text-heavy, repetitive, and easy to check. A manager preparing a status update, a recruiter drafting outreach messages, a marketer generating campaign variants, or an analyst cleaning up a report can all move faster because the machine handles the first pass. In those cases, AI does not merely make the worker faster; it changes the worker's bottleneck. Instead of spending energy on blank-page labor, the person spends more of it choosing, editing, and deciding what matters.

Quality is more complicated. In some settings, AI raises the floor by making acceptable work easier to produce. A rough writer can become more polished. A busy employee can produce a clearer memo. A team with limited bandwidth can respond more consistently to routine requests. The result is not always brilliance, but it is often better than what would have been produced under time pressure without assistance. That can be a real improvement, especially in organizations where mediocre communication, incomplete documentation, and delayed follow-up are constant sources of friction.

At the same time, AI can also flatten quality if people use it as a substitute for thought rather than a tool for thought. The model is good at sounding coherent, which can tempt users to accept the first draft because it looks finished. But a polished sentence is not the same thing as a correct one, and a smooth report is not the same thing as a good analysis. The quality gains come when AI helps a person explore more options, catch more errors, and spend more attention on the parts that require judgment. The quality losses come when teams mistake speed for rigor and volume for insight.

The speed effect is the most visible, and often the most seductive. AI shortens the distance between intention and output. A user can ask for a summary, a rewrite, a code suggestion, or a set of alternatives and receive something usable almost immediately. That immediacy changes expectations inside organizations. Once people get used to getting a draft in minutes, a process that takes days begins to feel slow, even if the final decision still requires human review. Over time, this can reshape the tempo of meetings, approvals, customer responses, and internal coordination. The work does not always become simpler, but it becomes more compressed.

Speed, however, has a second effect: it changes what counts as enough. When a team can generate ten versions of a proposal in the time it used to take to make one, the problem shifts from producing content to choosing among options. That sounds like a gain, and often it is. But it also means more output arrives at the point of decision, which can create a new burden of comparison and filtering. The human advantage moves upstream and downstream at once. People spend less time drafting and more time evaluating, but they also risk drowning in choices if they do not set clear standards for what good looks like.

In business settings, these three changes—productivity, quality, and speed—rarely move in isolation. Faster work can improve throughput, but only if the organization can absorb the output. Better first drafts can raise quality, but only if someone reviews them carefully. Higher productivity can lower costs, but it can also raise expectations, because once a task becomes easy to produce, leaders tend to ask for more of it. That is one reason AI adoption can feel less like a single efficiency gain and more like a rebalancing of the entire workflow. The machine does not simply replace effort; it redistributes effort toward coordination, oversight, and judgment.

There is also a subtle but important shift in what workers are valued for. In many roles, the scarce skill is no longer raw production of text, slides, or code. It is the ability to define the problem clearly, evaluate the output quickly, and know when the machine is helping versus misleading. That is why generative AI often rewards people who already understand their domain well. The better the human can specify the task and recognize a weak result, the more the tool amplifies performance. Recent research on generative AI adoption in knowledge work points to this pattern: benefits depend not only on the tool itself, but on how individuals and organizations integrate it into existing practices [32].

So the real change is not that AI makes everyone instantly more productive in the same way. It is that it changes where productivity comes from. Less time goes to routine production, more to review and refinement. Less value sits in producing a first draft, more in directing the process and deciding what deserves trust. In that sense, AI does not just accelerate work. It changes the balance between doing and deciding, and that balance is where the deeper transformation begins.

Why some jobs shrink while others are redefined

Jobs rarely disappear in one piece. More often, they come apart task by task. When a tool can draft routine messages, sort incoming requests, summarize documents, or generate a first pass at analysis, the pressure does not fall evenly across an occupation. It falls hardest on the parts that are repetitive, text-heavy, and easy to standardize. Those are the tasks most likely to shrink, not because they are unimportant, but because they can be produced cheaply and quickly by software that is good at pattern completion. The result is not always immediate layoffs. Sometimes it is fewer entry-level openings, thinner teams, or the same amount of work being handled by fewer people.

That is one reason the labor market response to AI is uneven. Some roles contain a large share of tasks that can be automated or accelerated; others contain only a small share. A legal assistant, a marketing coordinator, a customer support agent, and a financial analyst may all use AI, but not in the same way or to the same degree. In some jobs, the most routine work gets stripped away first, leaving a narrower core of judgment, relationship management, and accountability. In others, AI becomes a force multiplier that lets one person do more without changing the basic shape of the role. Research on AI and automation continues to point to this uneven pattern: the technology tends to disrupt specific task bundles rather than erase every job in a category at once [65].

As lower-value tasks shrink, the center of gravity inside a job often shifts. A manager may spend less time editing status reports and more time interpreting them. A recruiter may spend less time screening resumes and more time talking with finalists. A teacher may spend less time drafting worksheets and more time diagnosing where students are stuck. The job still exists, but the balance changes. What was once the bulk of the work becomes background support for a smaller number of decisions that require judgment, context, or trust. In that sense, AI does not just automate labor; it changes what the human part of the job is supposed to be.

This redefinition can make some workers more valuable, but it can also make the work more demanding. When software handles the draft, the search, or the first filter, the human is often expected to review more output, catch more errors, and make faster decisions. That can raise productivity while also raising the standard for what counts as competent performance. A person who once needed to produce one polished deliverable a day may now be expected to review ten machine-generated drafts and choose the best one. The work looks lighter from the outside, but the cognitive load can shift upward rather than disappear.

Jobs shrink when the tasks that once justified multiple people become compressible into fewer hours or fewer roles. Jobs are redefined when AI removes the mechanical middle of the work and leaves behind the parts that are harder to automate: judgment, negotiation, accountability, empathy, and coordination. That is why occupations built around direct human relationships tend to change differently from occupations built around information processing. A nurse, a sales leader, a project manager, or a therapist may use AI to prepare, organize, or document, but the core of the role still depends on human presence and responsibility.

By contrast, a role whose main value lies in turning one form of text into another is more exposed to being trimmed, split apart, or absorbed into a broader workflow.

There is also a status effect inside this shift. The tasks most vulnerable to automation are often the ones that junior workers used to learn first. If AI takes over the initial draft, the basic research pass, or the first round of sorting, organizations may gain speed but lose a traditional training path. That can make the pipeline thinner over time. Workers may enter a field with less hands-on practice and fewer chances to build intuition through repetition. The occupation survives, but the ladder into it becomes less stable. This is one reason analysts warn that labor-market disruption from AI is not only about job loss; it is also about how work is distributed, learned, and advanced inside firms and professions [33].

The clearest dividing line is not between "AI jobs" and "non-AI jobs." It is between work that can be decomposed into repeatable outputs and work that depends on a human being able to notice what the instructions missed. The first kind is easier to shrink. The second is easier to redefine. In practice, many jobs contain both. That is why the near-term effect of AI is often less dramatic than a headline about replacement suggests, yet more consequential than a simple productivity boost implies. It changes who does the routine work, who supervises the output, and how much of a role remains distinctly human once the machine has taken over the first draft.

Skills that become more valuable in an AI-rich workplace

In an AI-rich workplace, the most valuable people are not necessarily the ones who can produce the most text, the fastest spreadsheet, or the cleanest first draft. Those abilities still matter, but they are no longer scarce in the same way. What becomes more valuable is the capacity to decide what should be done, shape the problem clearly, and judge whether the machine's output is useful, misleading, incomplete, or simply off target. As AI takes over more of the mechanical and repeatable parts of knowledge work, human advantage shifts toward the parts that require direction, interpretation, and accountability.

One of the first skills to rise in value is problem framing. A generic request usually produces a generic result. A well-framed request, by contrast, can turn the same tool into something far more useful. That means workers who understand the business context, the audience, the constraints, and the desired outcome will get better results than workers who simply ask AI to "help." In practice, this is less about writing clever prompts than about knowing what matters. The person who can define the real question often outperforms the person who can only generate more material.

Judgment becomes more important for the same reason. Generative systems are good at producing plausible answers, but plausible is not the same as correct, relevant, or strategically wise. A worker who can quickly spot weak reasoning, missing context, unsupported claims, or a tone that does not fit the situation becomes a crucial filter between raw output and real value. This is especially true in fields where a small mistake can have outsized consequences. The more AI speeds up drafting and analysis, the more valuable it becomes to have people who can slow down at the right moment and ask, "Should this be trusted, revised, or discarded?"

Another skill that gains weight is domain expertise. AI can imitate patterns, but it does not possess lived familiarity with a company's customers, a hospital's workflow, a school's culture, or a regulator's expectations. That means the people who know the details of a field are in a stronger position than ever to guide AI use. They can tell when a suggestion sounds right but misses the practical reality. They can also train others in what good work looks like. Research on organizational AI adoption has consistently emphasized that the effects depend heavily on how systems are integrated into work design, worker experience, and existing practices [3].

Communication also becomes more valuable, but in a different form than before. When AI can draft a message, the human edge is not merely in writing polished sentences. It is in choosing the right level of directness, anticipating how different stakeholders will react, and aligning words with purpose. That includes explaining decisions, negotiating tradeoffs, and translating between technical possibilities and business needs. In many workplaces, the ability to turn AI-generated material into something clear, credible, and appropriate will matter more than the ability to generate the first version from scratch.

Adaptability is another premium skill. The tools are changing quickly, and so are the workflows around them. A worker who can learn a new system, test it, compare it with the old method, and adjust without waiting for a perfect playbook will have an advantage over someone who resists every change until it is forced on them. This does not mean chasing every new product. It means developing a habit of experimentation: trying small uses, noticing where the tool helps or fails, and refining the process. In early workplace studies of generative AI, the most immediate effects have often been uneven and task-specific rather than uniformly transformative, which makes learning-by-doing especially important [68].

Equally important is the ability to coordinate human and machine labor. As AI becomes a routine collaborator, workers need to know which parts of a task to delegate, which parts to keep under direct human control, and where handoffs create risk. That requires process thinking. It is not enough to ask whether AI can do something; the better question is whether involving AI improves the whole workflow. People who can redesign sequences of work, reduce rework, and build checks into the process will be especially valuable because they make the technology usable at scale, not just impressive in a demo.

Finally, trust-building becomes a core skill. In any setting where AI is used to support decisions, people will still want to know who is responsible, how the output was checked, and whether the system was used appropriately. The workers who can earn confidence from colleagues, clients, and managers by being transparent about limits and careful about quality will stand out. In an environment where software can generate confident-looking output on demand, the human reputation for reliability, discretion, and sound judgment becomes a stronger asset, not a weaker one.

CHAPTER 5

Chapter 5: The New Business Playbook

For many organizations, the first real question is not whether AI can be used, but where it can create measurable value without disrupting the work that already keeps the business running. That is why the conversation quickly moves beyond isolated tools and toward the structure of the business itself: how information moves, where delays accumulate, which tasks are repetitive enough to standardize, and where human judgment still matters most. In practice, the companies that benefit earliest are often not the ones that add the most features, but the ones that see AI as a way to reshape how work gets done.

Where AI creates immediate business value

The first places AI creates business value are usually not the most glamorous ones. They are the slow, repetitive, document-heavy parts of an organization where small gains compound across many employees and many transactions. A tool that shortens a support reply, drafts a proposal, summarizes a meeting, or extracts information from a form may not look revolutionary in isolation. But if those tasks happen thousands of times a week, the value shows up quickly in saved time, fewer bottlenecks, and faster movement through the work that matters most.

That is why the earliest wins often appear in functions where language is central and the output has a fairly standard shape: customer service, sales support, marketing, internal communications, basic research, and software development. In these settings, generative AI can produce a first draft, a structured summary, a response suggestion, or a set of options that a human then refines. The point is not that the machine finishes the job perfectly. The point is that it removes the most time-consuming middle layer. Organizations do not need every task to become fully automated for the economics to improve. They need enough of the routine work to be compressed that people can spend more of their time on judgment, exceptions, and relationship-heavy problems.

There is a reason this pattern repeats across industries. Generative AI tends to deliver the clearest return when the task is frequent, text-based, and easy to evaluate at least in its first pass. That makes it especially useful in work that is already standardized but still labor-intensive. A customer support team can use AI to classify incoming requests and draft responses. A sales team can use it to tailor outreach and prepare account notes. A legal or compliance team can use it to scan, summarize, and compare documents before a human reviews the result. A software team can use it to generate boilerplate code, explain unfamiliar code, or draft tests. Research on organizational AI adoption consistently points to this pattern: the strongest early effects come where the system can be embedded into existing routines rather than introduced as a flashy standalone tool [3].

The immediate value is not just speed. It is also consistency. Many businesses lose time because work arrives unevenly, gets handled differently by different people, or depends too much on who happens to be available. AI can help smooth those variations. It can provide a standard starting point, reduce the number of blank-page moments, and make output more uniform across teams. That matters in large organizations, where even a modest improvement in first-pass quality can reduce rework downstream. If a draft is closer to usable the first time, managers review less, employees revise less, and customers wait less. Those are ordinary gains, but they are powerful because they accumulate invisibly inside existing workflows.

Another reason AI creates immediate value is that it scales without requiring the same kind of linear staffing growth that traditional service models do. A company can use the same underlying system to assist many employees at once, across many locations and time zones. That does not eliminate the need for people; it changes where people are most valuable. Instead of adding headcount to handle every increase in volume, firms can use AI to absorb part of the load and reserve human effort for the cases that are messy, sensitive, or strategically important. This is especially attractive in functions where demand rises and falls unpredictably. The business value comes from flexibility as much as from raw efficiency.

Software engineering offers a clear example of how this works in practice. Developers do not usually adopt AI because they want a machine to replace their thinking. They adopt it because it can speed up the tedious parts of the job: generating scaffolding, suggesting code, explaining errors, and drafting tests. Studies of generative AI adoption in software work show that the benefits depend not only on the tool itself, but on how it fits into individual habits, team norms, and the surrounding technical environment [32]. That is true across business functions. A tool produces value fastest when it fits the way people already work, when the output is easy to check, and when the organization is willing to redesign the surrounding process instead of simply adding one more layer of software on top.

The most important point is that immediate business value usually comes from redesigning the workflow around the machine's strengths.

Companies that treat AI as a sidecar tend to get modest gains. Companies that use it to change the flow of work can get much more. That may mean routing routine inquiries to an AI assistant before a human sees them, using the model to prepare a first draft before review, or letting it handle the low-risk variations while staff focus on exceptions. The value is not only in what the tool does directly. It is in how it changes the shape of work: fewer handoffs, shorter delays, and more attention available for the decisions that still require a person.

How to redesign workflows instead of layering on tools

Adding AI to a workflow is easy. Redesigning the workflow so AI actually improves it is harder, but far more valuable. The difference is not cosmetic. A layered-on tool usually sits beside the existing process: people keep doing the same handoffs, approvals, and document shuffling, only now they also consult a chatbot or paste text into a generator. That can save a few minutes, but it often leaves the slowest and most frustrating parts of the process untouched. A redesigned workflow asks a different question: if a capable machine can draft, summarize, classify, search, or compare at high speed, which steps still need to exist, which steps can be merged, and which steps should move to a human only when judgment is required?

This matters because many organizations do not actually have a "writing problem" or a "research problem." They have a coordination problem. Information arrives in one place, gets retyped into another, waits for review, gets reformatted for a different audience, and then is checked again because no one trusts the chain. AI can help at each of those points, but only if the process is designed around where the machine is strong and where people remain essential. In manufacturing, digital transformation has long been tied to gains in productivity and quality when systems are integrated rather than merely added on top of existing routines [74]. The same logic applies here: value comes from changing the flow, not just decorating it with a new interface.

The first step is to map the work as it actually happens. Not the official version in the policy manual, but the real sequence of actions people take to get something done. Where does a request enter? Who touches it first? What information is missing most often? Where do people spend time copying, checking, or rewriting the same material? Those are the seams where AI can do useful work. A support team, for example, may not need AI to answer every customer question end-to-end. It may need AI to sort incoming messages, draft a first response, pull relevant case history, and flag the ones that require escalation. That is a workflow redesign: fewer interruptions, less duplication, and clearer handoff points.

It also helps to separate tasks that benefit from speed from tasks that require accountability. AI is well suited to the first draft, the first pass, and the first sort. Humans are still needed for exceptions, tradeoffs, and decisions that carry consequences. In practice, that means designing a process where the machine handles volume and the person handles judgment. A manager does not need to review every line of every report if the system can assemble a clean summary and highlight anomalies. A lawyer does not need to start from a blank page if AI can organize background material and prepare a rough outline. A teacher does not need to manually create every practice question if AI can generate variations for review. The workflow should route the right work to the right actor at the right moment.

This is why "human in the loop" should not become a vague slogan. If the human is only asked to approve a finished output after the fact, the process may still be fragile. A better design gives people leverage earlier, when they can shape the prompt, constrain the output, or define the criteria the system should use. That reduces rework later. In education and training settings, for example, practical guides increasingly emphasize not just tool use but the need to decide when AI supports learning and when it should be withheld to preserve the skill being developed [39]. The same principle applies in business: if AI is inserted at the wrong point, it can accelerate the wrong thing.

Organizations often make the mistake of measuring adoption by the number of licenses purchased or the number of employees who have tried a tool. Those numbers can be misleading. A better test is whether the process itself became simpler, faster, or more reliable. Did the cycle time shrink? Did the number of back-and-forth revisions fall? Did people spend less time on repetitive formatting and more time on judgment, customer contact, or strategic work? In small and medium-sized firms, research on automation and AI integration suggests that the real gains come when technology is embedded into the broader stack rather than treated as a standalone add-on [73]. The same is true in larger organizations, even if the scale is different.

Redesign also means accepting that some workflows should be broken apart and rebuilt from scratch. Legacy processes often exist because no one could do better with the tools available at the time. AI changes that constraint. A monthly reporting cycle that once required several days of manual assembly might become a living dashboard with AI-generated narrative updates. A proposal process that once moved through a long sequence of drafts might become a structured collaboration between subject matter experts and a model that prepares tailored versions for different audiences. When that happens, the organization is not simply working faster. It is working in a different shape.

The biggest temptation is to let every team experiment in isolation. That can produce useful ideas, but it also creates a patchwork of disconnected tools, duplicated effort, and inconsistent standards.

Workflow redesign works best when leaders define a few shared rules: what data can be used, where review is mandatory, what kinds of output require verification, and which steps should be standardized across teams. Without that discipline, AI becomes another layer of complexity. With it, AI can remove friction from the places where work has accumulated the most waste.

The role of leadership in adoption and governance

Leadership matters because adoption is not just a technology decision; it is an organizational decision about priorities, risk, pace, and accountability. The same tool can produce very different results depending on whether leaders treat it as a novelty, a cost-cutting device, or a capability that must be woven into how the organization actually works. In practice, the biggest barrier is rarely access to software. It is confusion about who is allowed to use it, for what purposes, under what standards, and with what oversight. When those questions are left vague, employees improvise. Some use AI freely, some avoid it entirely, and others use it in ways that save time but create hidden exposure.

That is why leadership sets the tone long before a formal policy is written. If executives talk about AI only as a threat to be contained, people will hide their use or wait passively for instructions. If leaders talk about it only as a productivity miracle, people may rush to adopt it without thinking through quality, privacy, or reputational risk. The more effective stance is neither fear nor hype. It is disciplined curiosity: encourage experimentation, but make clear that speed does not remove responsibility. Employees need to know that using AI is permitted, expected in some contexts, and bounded by rules that protect customers, data, and the organization's credibility.

Good governance begins with clarity about where AI belongs and where it does not. Not every task should be automated, and not every draft should be treated as ready simply because it was generated quickly. Leaders need to identify the categories of work where AI can assist, the categories where it can advise but not decide, and the categories where human judgment must remain primary. That distinction is especially important in work that involves legal exposure, financial commitments, personal data, medical information, hiring, discipline, or public communication. In those areas, "use AI" is not a meaningful instruction unless it comes with boundaries, review requirements, and named owners.

Leadership also has to decide whether adoption will be bottom-up, top-down, or both. Bottom-up experimentation often reveals the most useful applications because employees know where the friction lives. They see the repetitive requests, the document bottlenecks, the meeting overload, and the handoffs that consume time without adding much value. But bottom-up use alone can produce a patchwork of inconsistent practices. Top-down direction supplies standards, shared tools, and a common language for risk. The strongest organizations usually combine the two: they allow teams to test uses locally while leaders define guardrails, approve core platforms, and create a path for scaling what works.

This is also where governance becomes a management discipline rather than a legal afterthought. A policy is not enough if no one is responsible for implementation. Leaders need ownership structures: who approves new use cases, who reviews output quality, who handles incidents, who trains staff, and who updates rules as the technology changes. Without that structure, AI governance becomes symbolic—an ethics statement on a website, a memo no one reads, or a checklist completed once and forgotten. The point is not to create bureaucracy for its own sake. The point is to make sure the organization can answer basic questions when something goes wrong: Who used the tool? What data went in? What was checked? What was sent out? Who had final responsibility?

Another leadership challenge is culture. People adopt AI faster when they feel safe admitting uncertainty and asking for help. If managers reward only speed, employees may overuse AI to produce polished output that has not been properly reviewed. If managers punish any mistake involving AI, employees may stop experimenting altogether and the organization loses the chance to learn. The better culture is one of supervised learning: try, evaluate, correct, and improve. That means managers should talk openly about where AI saved time, where it failed, and what was learned. It also means they should model the behavior they expect from others by checking outputs, questioning assumptions, and refusing to outsource judgment.

Research on AI in organizations increasingly points to this human side of adoption: the effects of these systems depend not only on the tool itself, but on how work is designed, how employees experience the change, and how decision-making is shared between people and machines [3]. In other words, leadership is not just deciding whether AI enters the company; it is deciding what kind of company AI will help create. That includes whether AI reduces drudgery or simply raises output pressure, whether it broadens participation or concentrates authority, and whether it becomes a source of learning or a source of confusion. The organizations that handle this well do not treat governance as a brake on innovation. They treat it as the mechanism that makes broad adoption possible without losing control of the work itself.

Why speed of experimentation matters more than perfection

The temptation in a new technology cycle is to wait until the best version arrives. That instinct makes sense in ordinary procurement: if a tool is expensive, fragile, or hard to reverse, caution is wise. But AI adoption does not behave like a one-time purchase. It behaves more like a moving target. The value is not only in the current capability of the tool, but in how quickly an organization learns where it helps, where it fails, and where it should be redesigned out of the process altogether. In that environment, perfection becomes a trap. By the time a team finishes designing the ideal rollout, the tool, the market, or the workflow may already have changed.

Speed matters because the first experiment is rarely the final design. In practice, the early use of AI is less about getting everything right than about reducing uncertainty. A small pilot can reveal which tasks are easy wins, which require human review, and which are better left untouched. It can also expose the hidden costs that are easy to miss from the outside: extra editing, inconsistent outputs, compliance concerns, employee confusion, or the need for new approval steps. Those lessons are not side effects. They are the main product of experimentation. A company that experiments quickly learns faster than a company that debates in circles, and in a fast-moving market, learning is an operational advantage.

This is why many of the most successful AI uses begin as narrow, low-risk trials. A team may test AI on internal summaries, first-draft emails, customer support macros, or document classification before touching customer-facing decisions. The goal is not to prove that AI can do everything. The goal is to find where it reliably saves time or improves quality without creating new bottlenecks. That kind of testing is especially important because AI performance often depends on context. A model that works well for one department, one kind of document, or one style of prompt may perform very differently somewhere else. Small experiments make those differences visible before they become expensive.

There is also a deeper organizational reason to move quickly. When people see AI only as a future project, they tend to imagine a clean handoff: first the strategy, then the tool, then the transformation. Real adoption is messier. Employees learn by using the system, comparing its output with their own judgment, and gradually discovering where it fits. That learning cannot be fully designed in advance because much of it is tacit. It comes from the practical friction of use. A legal team may discover that AI is useful for summarizing contracts but not for final review. A sales team may find that it speeds up prospecting but needs guardrails around tone and accuracy. These insights emerge from contact with the work, not from abstract planning alone.

The risk of waiting for perfection is that it often protects the old workflow more than the organization. A perfect system is usually imagined as one that is accurate, secure, compliant, easy to use, and universally accepted before anyone touches it. But those standards are rarely met all at once by any new capability. If leaders demand complete certainty before experimenting, they end up preserving familiar inefficiencies while competitors learn in public. That matters because AI advantages compound. The organization that starts earlier gains more practice, more internal expertise, more data about what works, and more confidence in where to invest next. The advantage is not just the tool itself; it is the speed at which the organization becomes competent with the tool.

This is also where governance becomes practical rather than theoretical. Good governance does not mean freezing adoption until every risk is eliminated. It means setting boundaries that make experimentation safe enough to learn from. That may include defining approved use cases, requiring human review for sensitive outputs, limiting the kinds of data employees can enter, and creating a simple process for reporting failures. Those controls do not slow experimentation; they make it sustainable. An organization that can test quickly without creating chaos is in a far stronger position than one that either rushes blindly or waits indefinitely.

The broader pattern is familiar in other kinds of technological change: the winners are often not the ones with the most polished first version, but the ones that learn fastest from imperfect versions. AI is especially unforgiving of delay because the technology itself improves through use, feedback, and iteration. As teams interact with these systems, they develop better prompts, better review habits, and better ideas for redesigning work around what the software actually does well. That kind of adaptation cannot be purchased off the shelf. It has to be built through repeated, disciplined experimentation. The real question is not whether an AI tool is flawless on day one. It is whether an organization can learn faster than the pace of change around it.

CHAPTER 6

Chapter 6: Education, Learning, and the Future of Knowledge

Education is one of the first places where generative AI forces a deeper question: if a machine can draft, explain, summarize, and revise on command, what exactly is a student being asked to learn? The answer is not simply that old habits become obsolete, but that the boundaries between studying, producing, and demonstrating knowledge begin to blur. A tool that can help write an essay or untangle a difficult concept can also make it harder to tell whether a student understands the material or has only assembled a convincing result.

How AI changes what it means to study and write

Generative AI changes studying first by changing the cost of getting unstuck. A student no longer has to sit alone with a blank page, a confusing paragraph, or a half-formed idea and wait for inspiration to arrive. The system can explain a concept in simpler language, suggest a structure, generate examples, or offer a first draft that gives the student something concrete to react to. That makes studying feel less like a solitary struggle and more like an interactive process. The machine can act as a patient tutor, a brainstorming partner, or a rewriting assistant, depending on what the student needs at the moment.

That convenience is real, but it also changes the meaning of effort. In traditional study, a student often proves understanding by producing something from memory and judgment alone. With AI present, the student can produce a polished answer without fully owning the thinking behind it. The visible output may look strong even when the internal grasp is weak. This is why the old markers of academic performance become less reliable. A clean essay, a fluent summary, or a neat set of notes no longer tells you very much about whether the student can explain the material independently, connect it to other ideas, or use it under pressure.

This is one reason plagiarism has become harder to define and harder to police. The issue is no longer limited to copying from a source and pretending the words are one's own. A student might ask a model to draft a response, then revise it lightly, change a few phrases, and submit the result. The final text may be original in a narrow sense, but the thinking process behind it may be outsourced in a way that defeats the purpose of the assignment. Recent scholarship has noted that generative AI is forcing a rethinking of plagiarism, authorship, and intellectual property in academic writing [18]. The deeper problem is not simply rule-breaking; it is that the boundary between assistance and substitution has become blurry.

For students, that blur creates a new kind of temptation. If the machine can generate a passable answer in seconds, it becomes easier to skip the uncomfortable parts of learning: struggling through a difficult reading, organizing an argument, or rewriting a weak draft until it becomes clear. But those difficult parts are often where learning happens. Writing is not just a way to display knowledge; it is one of the main ways knowledge gets built. When a student uses AI only to avoid effort, the result may be a faster assignment but a thinner education. The work is done, yet the mind has not been stretched in the same way.

At the same time, it would be a mistake to treat AI use as automatically harmful. A model can help students study more effectively if it is used to test understanding rather than replace it. It can turn a dense chapter into simpler language, generate quiz questions, compare two interpretations of a passage, or help a student see whether an argument has gaps. In that role, AI becomes a kind of study partner that supports repetition, explanation, and revision. The difference lies in whether the student is using the tool to think more deeply or merely to produce text more quickly.

Writing, in particular, is shifting from a solitary act of composition to a more layered process of prompting, evaluating, revising, and verifying. Students may begin with rough ideas, ask the model for alternatives, compare versions, and then decide what fits the assignment and their own voice. That can be a useful skill in itself. But it also means that good writing instruction now has to include judgment about the machine's output: what to keep, what to discard, what to fact-check, and what to rewrite in one's own terms. In an AI-enabled classroom, the ability to edit well may matter as much as the ability to draft quickly.

That shift also changes what teachers are assessing. If a model can produce a competent five-paragraph essay on demand, then assignments that only reward generic structure and surface fluency will tell educators less than they used to. The challenge is not simply to catch misuse, but to design work that reveals thought: oral defenses, in-class writing, process drafts, source comparisons, reflection on revisions, and assignments tied to specific class discussions or local evidence. Generative AI makes it easier to produce finished-looking work, which means education has to place more weight on the path to the answer, not just the answer itself. In that environment, studying and writing become less about showing that a machine can help and more about showing that the student can still reason, choose, and explain.

Personalized tutoring and adaptive learning at scale

Personalization is where generative AI moves from being a helpful tool to something closer to an always-available tutor. A student no longer has to wait for office hours, a study group, or a teacher's next explanation to get unstuck. The system can rephrase a concept in simpler language, slow down and walk through a problem step by step, or switch to a different example when the first one does not land. That matters because many learning bottlenecks are not caused by a lack of intelligence or effort. They come from timing. A learner hits confusion in the middle of a task, and the delay between confusion and help is what turns a small gap into a larger one.

What makes this different from older educational software is not just interactivity, but responsiveness. Traditional digital learning tools often followed a fixed path: watch this lesson, answer these questions, move to the next module. They could adapt in limited ways, but they rarely changed their teaching style in real time. Generative systems can do more than score an answer. They can respond to the student's language, estimate what kind of explanation might help, and adjust the level of detail on the fly. In practice, that means one student can get a compact overview, another can get a more patient walkthrough, and a third can get a fresh analogy that connects the material to something familiar.

This is why advocates see personalized tutoring as one of the most promising uses of the technology. A human tutor is still unmatched in many ways, but human tutoring is scarce and unevenly distributed. It is expensive, time-limited, and often available only to students who already have access to extra support. Generative AI can lower that barrier by offering a basic form of one-to-one guidance at far larger scale. That does not make it a replacement for teachers. It makes it a potentially powerful supplement, especially for practice, repetition, and explanation. Education researchers and higher education leaders have increasingly noted that these systems are forcing institutions to rethink long-standing assumptions about how learning support is delivered and who gets it [86].

The scale issue is important. A school, district, or university can only hire so many tutors, teaching assistants, or writing coaches. But a digital tutor can be present for thousands of learners at once, across different times of day and different subject areas. That opens the door to support that is not confined to the classroom calendar. A student can review algebra at night, ask for a simpler explanation before a quiz, or practice a language conversation repeatedly without feeling embarrassed about asking the same question again. The machine does not tire, lose patience, or treat repetition as a burden. For learners who hesitate to ask for help, that can make a real difference in whether they persist or give up.

Adaptive learning takes this one step further by using ongoing interaction to shape what happens next. If a student keeps missing the same kind of question, the system can slow down, change the sequence, or return to a prerequisite concept. If the student is moving quickly, it can raise the difficulty or offer more advanced practice. In theory, this makes instruction more efficient because it reduces both boredom and frustration. In practice, the value depends on how well the system is designed and how carefully it is used. A well-tuned tutor can help a learner spend more time on what they actually need. A poorly tuned one can overcorrect, oversimplify, or keep a student inside a narrow path that looks personalized but is really just automated repetition.

There is also a deeper shift in what "help" looks like. Many students do not need a machine to give them the answer. They need help getting started, seeing a structure, or recognizing what a good next step looks like. Generative AI is especially useful there because it can generate hints, prompts, outlines, and examples instead of only final responses. That changes the emotional experience of learning as much as the technical one. The blank page is less intimidating when a system can produce a starter draft. A hard reading becomes more manageable when the language can be translated into simpler terms. A dense concept becomes less opaque when the learner can ask for the same idea three different ways without social friction.

At the same time, personalization has limits that matter in education. A tutor that always adjusts to the learner can also make it easier to avoid productive struggle. Real learning often requires friction: the moment when a student has to wrestle with a problem long enough for understanding to form. If the system steps in too quickly, it may reduce the effort needed to answer a question while also reducing the effort needed to think. There is a difference between support and substitution. The best educational use of generative AI is not to remove difficulty altogether, but to make difficulty more usable. It should help students stay in the zone where they can still do the work themselves, with guidance, rather than outsourcing the work entirely.

That is why the most valuable implementations will likely be the ones that are designed around pedagogy rather than novelty. The question is not whether a system can chat with a student. The question is whether it can help that student learn more reliably, more equitably, and with less wasted time. In that sense, personalized tutoring at scale is not just a technology story. It is a distribution story. It asks whether high-quality explanation, feedback, and practice can become less dependent on geography, family resources, or institutional capacity. If that happens, the impact of AI in education will be measured not only by how much content it can generate, but by how many learners it can keep moving forward when they would otherwise stall.

Rethinking assessment in an AI-enabled classroom

Once AI can help students draft, revise, summarize, and brainstorm on demand, the old assumption that a finished assignment cleanly reveals what a student knows starts to break down. A polished essay may still be the product of careful thinking, but it may also be the result of a prompt, a few edits, and a machine's ability to produce fluent prose on cue. That does not make assessment irrelevant. It makes the purpose of assessment more important. If the tool can handle the visible surface of a task, then teachers have to ask what they actually want to measure: recall, understanding, reasoning, originality, persistence, or the ability to use tools responsibly.

This is why assessment in an AI-enabled classroom cannot rely as heavily on one-shot take-home products that are easy to outsource. A paper written entirely outside class used to serve as a reasonable proxy for student thinking because the act of writing itself was part of the evidence. Now the evidence is noisier. Students can use AI in ways that are helpful, harmful, invisible, or somewhere in between, and many do so because the line between support and substitution is not always clear to them. Research on college students suggests that use is already shaped by institutional policy, major, age, and other factors, which means the classroom is not facing a single uniform behavior but a wide range of habits and incentives [85].

The response is not to abandon writing, but to diversify what counts as evidence. In an AI-rich setting, assessment works better when it includes more than the final artifact. Teachers can look at outlines, drafts, annotations, revision notes, in-class writing, oral explanation, problem-solving steps, and short reflections on process. These forms of assessment make thinking visible in ways that a polished submission alone cannot. They also reduce the incentive to treat AI as a shortcut, because the student must show how the work developed, not just what the final version looks like.

That shift has a practical benefit: it gives instructors a better picture of student judgment. A student who uses AI well is not simply producing text faster. They are deciding what to ask, what to accept, what to reject, and how to verify the result. Those are real skills, and they matter in school as much as they do at work. A classroom that ignores AI entirely may miss an opportunity to teach those skills. A classroom that allows AI without changing assessment may reward output without understanding. The more useful middle ground is to design tasks where the student's reasoning remains visible even if a tool is involved.

Oral defense is one example. So is asking students to explain why they chose a source, why they revised a paragraph, or how they would improve an AI-generated draft that contains an error. Another useful approach is to assign work that depends on local context, class discussion, or personal analysis rather than generic information that any model can produce. When a prompt asks students to connect a concept to a specific lab result, a recent seminar, a neighborhood issue, or a case studied in class, it becomes harder for a machine-generated answer to stand in for genuine engagement without the student's own judgment.

Assessment also needs clearer norms. If students are expected to use AI in some settings and avoid it in others, the rules have to be explicit. Ambiguity invites both overuse and fear. Some students will lean on the tool because they assume everyone else is doing the same. Others will avoid it entirely because they worry about crossing an invisible line. Clear policies help separate acceptable assistance from inappropriate substitution. They also create room to teach citation, disclosure, and attribution in a way that reflects how knowledge work is changing. As scholarship on plagiarism and intellectual property has noted, generative systems have complicated older assumptions about authorship and ownership, especially when machine output blends with human revision [18].

What changes most, then, is not the value of assessment but its design. In an AI-enabled classroom, the strongest assessments are often the ones that ask students to do what machines still do poorly: explain choices, defend claims, connect ideas across contexts, and demonstrate learning over time. That does not mean every assignment must become a performance or an interrogation. It means teachers have to be more deliberate about matching the assignment to the learning goal. If the goal is to test whether a student can produce a clean prose draft, AI may blur the result. If the goal is to test whether the student can think, revise, and justify under real conditions, the assessment can be built to make that visible.

What students need to learn now to stay relevant

The most important thing students need to learn now is not how to outtype a machine or memorize facts that a machine can retrieve instantly. It is how to think clearly in the presence of a machine that can draft, search, summarize, and suggest at high speed. That means learning to ask better questions, define a problem before trying to solve it, and recognize when a polished answer is actually weak. In an AI-rich environment, the student who can frame an assignment well, test a claim, and compare alternatives will often do better than the student who can simply produce more words. The skill is shifting from output alone to judgment about output.

That shift changes what counts as academic strength. Writing still matters, but not as a race to generate text. Students now need to learn how to use writing as a thinking tool: to clarify a position, expose gaps in reasoning, and distinguish evidence from decoration. A machine can produce a fluent paragraph in seconds, but fluency is not the same as understanding. Students who rely on AI without checking the logic of what it gives them may end up with work that sounds competent while resting on shaky assumptions. The new baseline skill is not "can you produce a draft?" but "can you tell whether this draft is accurate, relevant, and proportionate to the task?"

Research on AI adoption in software engineering shows that use does not depend only on the tool itself; it also depends on the individual's habits, the surrounding technology, and the social setting in which the tool is used [32]. That lesson applies to students too. The same AI system can make one learner more independent and another more passive. A student who uses AI to generate practice questions, compare interpretations, or explain a concept in a different way is building competence. A student who uses it to bypass the hard part of reading, drafting, or revising may get faster results while learning less. The tool is not the whole story; the learning strategy around it is decisive.

Students also need stronger verification habits. If AI can produce a plausible answer on demand, then checking becomes a core literacy rather than an afterthought. That means tracing claims back to sources, noticing when a response sounds generic, and learning to ask for uncertainty, alternatives, or supporting evidence. It also means being comfortable with the fact that the first answer is often not the best answer. In practice, the student who learns to interrogate a machine's output—by asking what is missing, what is disputed, and what would change the answer—builds a more durable advantage than the student who accepts convenience at face value.

Another essential skill is task design. Many students still think of schoolwork as something handed down in a fixed form: read this, write that, solve this problem, submit it. But in an AI-enabled world, the ability to break a large assignment into smaller parts becomes increasingly valuable. A student who can separate brainstorming from drafting,

drafting from fact-checking, and fact-checking from polishing is better positioned to use AI well without becoming dependent on it. This is not just an efficiency trick. It is a way of preserving ownership over the thinking process while still benefiting from machine assistance. The more a student can name the purpose of each step, the less likely the tool is to blur the line between assistance and substitution.

Students should also learn to work across domains, not just within them. Generative AI is especially useful at connecting ideas, translating between styles, and producing variations. That makes broad literacy more important, not less. A student who understands history, statistics, communication, and basic technical concepts can ask better questions and spot better opportunities than a student who knows only one narrow lane. In an era when many routine tasks can be automated or accelerated, the ability to connect information across fields becomes a real advantage. It helps students adapt when job requirements shift, because the value is no longer only in knowing a subject, but in using knowledge flexibly.

Finally, students need to learn how to use AI without letting it erode their own voice or confidence. The temptation is to let the machine smooth out every rough edge, but rough edges are often where original thought begins. If a student always asks AI to rewrite, simplify, or complete ideas too early, the result can be technically clean and intellectually thin. Better habits include drafting before prompting, using AI to challenge an argument rather than replace it, and treating the system as a sparring partner instead of a substitute mind. The students who stay relevant will not be the ones who use AI the most. They will be the ones who use it with enough discipline to keep their own judgment intact while extending what they can do.

CHAPTER 7

Chapter 7: Everyday Life in the Age of Generative Intelligence

Generative intelligence is beginning to move out of the browser tab and into the texture of ordinary routines. It is showing up where people write, sort, compare, decide, and try to keep up with the steady flow of information that fills a day. That matters because everyday life is often shaped less by dramatic breakthroughs than by small acts of delegation: asking for a draft, a reminder, a summary, a suggestion, or a second opinion. The result is not simply faster completion of chores. It is a subtle change in how attention is managed, how choices are framed, and how much of one's mental effort is spent supervising tools rather than working from first principles.

AI as a daily assistant for writing, planning, and decision-making

For many people, the most visible change from generative AI is not a dramatic new system but a familiar one that has become easier to ask for help. Writing is often the first place this happens. A person can paste in a rough email, a half-finished memo, or a messy paragraph of notes and get back something cleaner, more formal, more concise, or better organized. The machine does not need to understand the whole situation the way a human colleague would. It only needs enough context to produce a useful draft. That makes it feel less like specialized software and more like a responsive assistant sitting on call.

This is why AI has spread so quickly into the ordinary mechanics of work and home life. It lowers the friction of starting. Instead of facing a blank page, people can ask for an outline, a first paragraph, a version in simpler language, or a rewrite for a different audience. In business settings, that might mean turning rough bullet points into a client update. At home, it might mean drafting a complaint letter, revising a résumé, or composing a message that sounds polite instead of abrupt. The value is not just speed. It is the way AI helps people move from intention to usable text with less effort and less hesitation.

Planning is another area where generative tools are becoming part of the daily routine. A calendar can tell you when something is due, but it cannot help you think through the shape of a week, the order of a project, or the tradeoffs among competing tasks. An AI assistant can. It can take a list of obligations and turn them into a schedule, a checklist, or a sequence of steps. It can suggest what to do first, what can wait, and what might be missing. That makes it useful not only for productivity but for mental organization. People often use it to externalize the clutter in their heads and turn vague pressure into something more manageable.

The same pattern shows up in decision-making, though here the role of the tool is more delicate. AI can help frame options, compare alternatives, and surface questions that a person might overlook. It can summarize the pros and cons of a choice, draft a decision memo, or generate scenarios for what might happen if a plan changes. In that sense, it acts less like a decision-maker than a structured thinking aid. Recent research on AI adoption in applied settings suggests that people are more likely to use these tools when they fit naturally into existing tasks and reduce effort without requiring major workflow changes [32]. That helps explain why AI is often adopted first as a helper in the background rather than as a system that announces itself as transformative.

But the convenience comes with an important shift in habit. When a tool is always available to draft, sort, and suggest, people may begin to rely on it before they have fully formed their own view. That can be useful when the task is routine and the stakes are low. It becomes riskier when the answer depends on context, values, or consequences that the system cannot truly evaluate. A good assistant can help you think, but it cannot know what matters most to you unless you make that clear. It can produce a polished recommendation that sounds complete while leaving out assumptions you would have noticed yourself. The more the output looks finished, the easier it is to accept too quickly.

That is why the most effective users treat AI as a drafting and organizing layer, not as an authority. They ask it to generate options, then they edit, compare, and verify. They use it to move faster through the mechanical parts of a task, not to replace the judgment that gives the task meaning. This is especially important in writing, where tone, audience, and purpose matter as much as sentence quality. A machine can imitate confidence and clarity, but it cannot decide whether a message should be blunt, cautious, diplomatic, or firm. Those choices belong to the person who owns the outcome.

In daily life, the real change is not that AI has made people unnecessary. It is that ordinary tasks now begin with a delegation step. Before writing, planning, or deciding, a person can ask the system for a starting point. That small shift changes the rhythm of work and thought. It can make people more productive, more organized, and less stuck. It can also make them less practiced at struggling through ambiguity on their own. The balance between those two effects will depend less on the tool itself than on how deliberately people use it.

How recommendation systems and generative tools shape attention

Recommendation systems and generative tools shape attention in related but distinct ways. Recommendation systems decide what rises to the top of a feed, a homepage, a search result, or a video queue. Generative tools decide what appears once a person asks for help, and increasingly they can also decide how that help is framed, shortened, expanded, or personalized. One system is primarily about selection; the other is about creation. Together, they influence not just what people see, but what they are likely to think is worth seeing, reading, or doing next. In that sense, they do not merely serve attention. They organize it.

The influence begins with a simple fact: attention is limited, and digital systems are designed to compete for it. Recommendation engines learn from clicks, watch time, dwell time, shares, and other signals that stand in for interest. They are optimized to keep people engaged, which often means showing more of what has already worked. That can be useful when the goal is to find a movie, a song, a product, or a tutorial. But it also creates a strong pull toward repetition, familiarity, and emotional intensity. Content that is surprising, provocative, or highly tailored can outperform content that is balanced, slow, or context-rich. Over time, the feed starts to feel less like a neutral window and more like a responsive environment that learns which buttons to press.

Generative tools add another layer because they can produce the content itself, not just sort it. If a recommendation system predicts what a person wants next, a generative system can manufacture a plausible next thing on demand. That means the boundary between discovery and fabrication starts to blur. A user may ask for a summary, a list of ideas, a headline, a product description, or a personalized explanation, and the system can generate something that feels tailored and immediate. The result is convenience, but also a subtle narrowing of friction. Friction used to serve as a signal. If finding information took effort, that effort sometimes prompted comparison, skepticism, or a pause. When the answer arrives instantly and in polished form, the user is more likely to accept it at face value or move on without checking alternatives.

This is one reason generative systems can be so effective at capturing and directing attention: they reduce the cost of producing endless variations. A platform no longer has to wait for a human writer, editor, or creator to make multiple versions of a message. It can generate many at once, test them, and keep the ones that perform best. In marketing and consumer settings, research has long shown that AI can be used to personalize and optimize engagement at scale [5]. The same basic logic now extends far beyond advertising. It can shape news summaries, shopping prompts, study aids, and even the tone of a virtual assistant. What matters is not only that the content is relevant, but that it is relevant in a way that keeps the interaction going.

That creates a powerful feedback loop. Recommendation systems learn which content holds attention. Generative tools supply more content in the style that seems to work. The more a person interacts, the more data the system gets about preferences, habits, and vulnerabilities. Then the system refines its next output. This is why the experience can feel eerily personal. It is not only that the system knows what topics you like. It may also learn whether you respond to urgency, reassurance, novelty, controversy, humor, or simplification. Once those patterns are visible, the system can present information in a way that feels almost custom-built for your mood and attention span.

The risk is not just distraction in the ordinary sense. It is attentional capture that becomes harder to notice because it arrives wrapped in usefulness. A recommendation feed can keep people scrolling. A generative assistant can keep them asking. A search interface can keep them inside a closed loop of increasingly tailored answers. The user may feel more efficient, but efficiency is not the same as breadth. If the system repeatedly surfaces what is easiest to consume, most likely to satisfy, or most likely to trigger another interaction, it can quietly reduce exposure to disagreement, depth, and surprise. The result is a kind of narrowing that feels like personalization.

At the same time, these tools are not inherently manipulative. They can help people focus, filter noise, and reduce overload. A well-designed recommender can surface relevant articles, useful courses, or practical products that a person would never have found alone. A generative tool can turn a messy information environment into something more usable and less exhausting. The issue is not whether these systems influence attention—they all do—but whether that influence is visible, accountable, and aligned with the user's goals. A system that serves attention well should help people decide what matters, not just what keeps them engaged.

That distinction becomes more important as generative systems move from optional tools to default interfaces. Once a machine is not only recommending what to look at but also drafting what to say, summarize, buy, or believe next, it becomes part of the architecture of attention itself. The practical question is no longer whether these systems are clever. It is whether they are helping people direct attention deliberately, or simply making it easier for attention to be captured, shaped, and sold.

The convenience tradeoff: speed versus dependence

The appeal of generative AI is easy to understand: it removes friction. A task that used to take ten minutes of drafting, searching, rewriting, or formatting can now be compressed into a few seconds of prompting and review. That speed is not a minor perk. It changes the emotional experience of work. People feel less stuck, less burdened by blank pages and repetitive chores, and more able to move from intention to output. In that sense, convenience is real value. It frees attention for higher-order judgment and makes ordinary tasks feel lighter.

But convenience is never free. The same systems that make a task easier can also make the user less practiced at doing it unaided. When a machine repeatedly supplies the first draft, the first answer, or the first plan, people begin to rely on its shape of thinking. They may still be involved, but their role shifts from creating to selecting, correcting, and approving. That shift can be efficient, especially when time is scarce. It can also create a subtle form of dependence: the user becomes faster at using the tool and slower at operating without it.

This is not just a matter of skill atrophy in the abstract. In daily life, dependence often shows up as a narrowing of initiative. A person who once wrote a rough email from scratch may now wait for a prompt before starting. Someone who used to outline a presentation mentally may now ask the system to generate options before deciding what they think. Over time, the tool becomes part of the cognitive opening move. That can be useful, but it also means the user's own ability to begin, structure, and revise may weaken if it is never exercised. Research on generative AI use has begun to describe this kind of cognitive offloading, where people shift mental work to the system and gradually change how ownership and responsibility feel in the process [96].

The tradeoff becomes sharper when the task matters. If the goal is to save time on a routine reply, dependence is a small price to pay. If the goal is to make a judgment under uncertainty, dependence can be dangerous. A tool that helps generate options can also make those options feel more complete than they are. Because the output arrives smoothly and confidently, users may stop checking the assumptions underneath it. In that moment, convenience can blur into complacency. The machine does not just speed up work; it can also lower the user's guard.

That is one reason the most responsible way to use generative AI is not to ask, "Can it do this faster?" but, "What happens to my ability if I let it do this often?" Some tasks are safe to offload almost completely because they are low stakes and easily verified. Others should be used as training wheels rather than substitutes. A student who asks for an outline can still learn structure if they compare the machine's version with their own. A manager who uses AI to draft a memo can still preserve judgment if they treat the draft as raw material, not authority. The danger is not assistance itself. The danger is assistance that quietly becomes replacement.

There is also a broader organizational effect. When many people in a workplace depend on the same system for drafting, summarizing, or deciding, the organization may gain speed but lose diversity of thought. Outputs begin to sound similar. Processes become easier to standardize. That can improve consistency, but it can also flatten originality and reduce the number of people who truly understand the work end to end. In high-pressure environments, this kind of dependence can spread because it feels efficient in the short run. Yet efficiency that weakens judgment creates a hidden cost that only becomes visible when something unusual happens.

The practical question, then, is not whether to use these tools. It is how to keep the convenience without surrendering too much capability. That requires a habit of staying in the loop: checking important outputs, occasionally doing the task by hand, and noticing when the tool is becoming a crutch rather than an aid. The point is not to resist speed for its own sake. It is to preserve enough independence that speed remains a choice rather than a necessity.

Practical habits for using AI without losing judgment

The safest way to use AI is not to ask it to think for you, but to make it work inside a habit of review. That sounds simple, yet it is the difference between a tool that extends judgment and a tool that quietly replaces it. The aim is not to avoid AI-generated drafts, summaries, or suggestions. The aim is to keep a human checkpoint at the moments where meaning, accuracy, and consequences matter. If a system helps you move faster, the question becomes whether you are still slowing down long enough to notice what it got wrong, what it left out, and what it assumed without being asked.

One useful habit is to separate generation from decision. Let the model produce options, but do not let its first answer become the final one by default. Treat the output as a working draft, not a verdict. This is especially important when the task involves judgment rather than formatting: choosing a strategy, evaluating a risk, summarizing a dispute, or explaining something to another person. AI is often strongest when it expands the range of possibilities. Human judgment is strongest when it narrows those possibilities into a choice that fits the real situation. The handoff between those two functions should be deliberate, not automatic.

Another habit is to ask the model to show its work in a form you can inspect. That does not mean trusting every explanation it gives; generative systems can produce neat reasoning that sounds convincing even when it is not grounded. But asking for assumptions, alternatives, or a step-by-step outline makes it easier to spot weak points. If you are using AI to draft an email, a report, or a plan, ask what it is assuming about audience, purpose, timing, and tone. If you are using it to compare options, ask it to list the tradeoffs rather than only the recommendation. This shifts the interaction from passive acceptance to active review.

It also helps to build a personal rule for verification. The more important the output, the more independent checking it deserves. A quick brainstorm may only need a glance. A summary used in a meeting may need a scan against the source material. A claim that will shape a decision, a policy, or a public statement should be checked against original documents or a second reliable source before it is used. This matters because polished language can disguise uncertainty, and because AI can be wrong in ways that are hard to notice if you are moving quickly. In practice, many users benefit from asking a simple question: What would I need to confirm before I would feel comfortable acting on this?

Another discipline is to keep a clear boundary around what you should not delegate. Some tasks are fine to accelerate; others are too tied to responsibility, trust, or context. If the output could affect money, health, compliance, reputation, or someone else's opportunities, AI should not be the last voice in the process. It may help with drafting, organizing, or generating a first pass, but the final call should remain with a person who understands the stakes. That boundary is not anti-AI. It is what makes AI usable in serious settings. In higher education, for example, guidance increasingly emphasizes that students and educators need AI literacy not just to use tools, but to know when to rely on them and when to eschew them altogether [39].

It is equally important to protect your own memory and understanding. If AI always supplies the next sentence, the next summary, or the next answer, it becomes easy to stop rehearsing the underlying skill. That is how convenience turns into dependence. A good habit is to do some work first, then use AI to compare, refine, or challenge it. Write the rough outline before asking for edits. Form your own answer before asking for alternatives. Make your own judgment before asking for a second opinion. This preserves the mental effort that builds competence. The machine can remove friction, but it should not remove the practice that makes you better at the task over time.

Finally, use AI in ways that leave an audit trail for yourself. Save the prompt, the version you used, and the parts you accepted or rejected when the stakes are more than trivial. This is not bureaucracy for its own sake. It helps you notice patterns in your own use: where the tool consistently helps, where it tends to overreach, and where you are too quick to trust a fluent answer. Over time, that record becomes a private map of your judgment. The point of using AI well is not to become more dependent on a machine's confidence. It is to become more disciplined about your own.

CHAPTER 8

Chapter 8: Power, Politics, and the Battle Over Control

Once AI becomes useful at scale, it stops being just another software feature and starts looking like infrastructure, which is why the struggle over it quickly moves from product design to power. The same systems that speed up writing, analysis, and decision-making also affect who gets to set the terms of access, whose information counts, and how much leverage large institutions can accumulate. In that sense, the debate is not only about what AI can do, but about who controls the systems that shape what others can do with it.

Why AI is becoming a strategic asset

AI becomes a strategic asset when it stops being treated as a convenient feature and starts being treated as a source of leverage. That shift matters because strategic assets do more than save time. They change what an organization can do faster than competitors, with less friction, and at a scale that would be difficult to match by hiring alone. In that sense, AI is not just another productivity tool sitting beside email or spreadsheets. It is increasingly part of the machinery that shapes how decisions are made, how knowledge moves, and how quickly an institution can respond to change.

One reason AI has this strategic quality is that it sits close to the core of knowledge work. Many organizations run on text, summaries, forecasts, reports, proposals, customer interactions, and internal documentation. Generative systems can now touch all of those flows. They can draft, translate, classify, retrieve, compare, and repackage information in ways that make the organization faster without necessarily making it larger. That is why the technology is spreading beyond isolated experiments and into business models, operating processes, and management routines [4]. The value is not only in the output the system produces, but in the reduction of delay between having information and acting on it.

Strategic value also comes from breadth. A narrow tool can improve one task; a general-purpose capability can influence many. AI can be used in customer service, marketing, research support, software development, training, procurement, legal review, and executive communication, often with the same underlying system adapted to different needs. That versatility makes it attractive to leaders because it can be deployed across departments rather than purchased for only one team. It also means the payoff compounds. If one group uses AI to produce a draft, another to review it, and a third to summarize feedback, the organization may gain not just speed, but a new rhythm of work.

There is another reason AI becomes strategic: it changes the balance between internal capability and external dependence. A company that can use AI well can do more with its existing people, but it can also become less reliant on outside vendors for routine analysis, content production, and first-pass problem solving. At the same time, firms that fail to build their own competence may find themselves dependent on platforms they do not control. That dependence can show up in pricing, access, data use, integration choices, and the pace at which the technology evolves. In other words, AI is strategic not only because it creates value, but because it can shift who has leverage in the relationship between buyer and provider.

This is where the issue moves from efficiency to power. A system that helps employees work faster can also help an organization see patterns sooner, scale decisions more consistently, and respond to customers or markets with less lag. Those advantages matter in competitive industries, but they matter just as much inside government, education, healthcare, media, and finance, where information advantages affect outcomes well beyond profit. Recent surveys of generative AI applications show how quickly these systems have spread across domains, which is one reason policymakers and institutions are increasingly trying to classify and govern them as a distinct category rather than as a passing software trend [48].

AI is also strategic because it can be embedded. Once a model is connected to workflows, databases, communication systems, and decision rules, it becomes harder to separate from the organization's core operations. That creates a kind of institutional stickiness. A company that redesigns its intake process around AI-assisted triage, or its content pipeline around AI-assisted drafting, may gain efficiency that is difficult for competitors to copy quickly. But the reverse is also true: if the system is poorly chosen or poorly governed, the organization can become locked into a process that is fast but brittle, or cheap but unreliable. Strategic assets create advantage only when they are managed with discipline.

For leaders, the deeper implication is that AI is not simply a tool to be adopted at the edge of the business. It is a capability that can influence the center of gravity. It affects how knowledge is produced, who can act on it, and how much judgment remains human at each step. In a period when digital transformation is reshaping business models and organizational structures across sectors, generative AI is becoming one of the most consequential forms of that transformation because it reaches into work that was once thought to be too interpretive, too creative, or too specialized to automate meaningfully [34]. The organizations that recognize this early are not just buying software. They are deciding where future leverage will come from.

The tension between innovation and regulation

The tension between innovation and regulation is built into the technology itself. Generative AI is not a single product that can be approved, monitored, and then left alone. It is a moving system: models improve, interfaces change, new uses emerge, and capabilities spill into areas that policymakers did not anticipate when the first rules were drafted. That creates a basic mismatch. Innovation rewards speed, experimentation, and broad deployment. Regulation rewards caution, clarity, and accountability. The two goals are not enemies, but they do pull in opposite directions.

That pull is especially strong because AI is useful in so many different settings at once. A system that helps a marketer draft copy can also help a student write an essay, a clinician summarize notes, a recruiter screen résumés, or a programmer produce code. Each use case raises different concerns. A tool that is harmless in one context may be risky in another. This makes AI harder to regulate than older technologies that were easier to define by industry or by device. Instead of asking whether AI should be allowed, governments and institutions have to ask where it should be allowed, under what conditions, and with what safeguards.

The pressure to innovate comes from more than curiosity. It comes from competition. Companies fear that if they move too slowly, rivals will release a better model, capture users, and set the standard for the market. That fear is not imaginary. In fast-moving markets, delays can look like weakness, and a cautious rollout can be punished by investors, customers, or employees who expect the next improvement to arrive immediately. At the same time, a rushed release can expose users to unreliable outputs, privacy problems, or misuse. The result is a recurring dilemma: move fast and risk harm, or move slowly and risk irrelevance.

Regulation enters that conflict because AI systems do not simply create value; they also create exposure. Organizations may depend on them for decisions, content generation, or customer interactions without fully understanding how the system reached a result or what data it absorbed along the way. That makes oversight difficult. Traditional regulatory tools often assume that the regulated object is stable and visible. But generative systems can be updated frequently, tuned for different customers, or embedded inside larger products in ways that make responsibility harder to trace. Recent policy research shows that governments are already telling a familiar set of stories about AI—innovation, competitiveness, risk, ethics, and sovereignty—but those narratives do not automatically resolve the practical problem of governing systems that evolve faster than public institutions do [50].

There is also a deeper issue: regulation is not only about stopping harm after it appears. It is about shaping the incentives that determine what gets built in the first place. If rules are too vague, companies may interpret them as permission to move ahead and sort out consequences later. If rules are too rigid, they may lock in old assumptions and discourage useful experimentation. That is why the most effective governance tends to focus less on banning an entire class of tools and more on setting expectations for testing, disclosure, documentation, human oversight, and accountability. The goal is not to freeze the technology. The goal is to make sure progress does not depend on ignoring its side effects.

This is where transparency becomes central. People cannot meaningfully trust systems they cannot inspect at all, especially when those systems influence hiring, lending, education, health, or public communication. But transparency is not a magic answer either. Revealing everything about a model is not always possible, and even when technical details are available, most users cannot interpret them directly. That is why standards and frameworks matter: they translate abstract concerns into operational requirements that organizations can actually follow, such as documenting model behavior, explaining intended use, and reporting limitations [35]. In practice, regulation works best when it asks not for perfect certainty, but for visible responsibility.

The broader challenge is that both sides of the debate are partly right. Innovation does bring real gains in productivity, creativity, and access. It can make knowledge work faster, lower barriers to entry, and open up new forms of service and learning. But regulation is responding to a real problem too: powerful systems can scale mistakes just as easily as they scale benefits. A flawed output repeated thousands of times is not a small flaw. It is a systematic one. The question, then, is not whether society should choose innovation or regulation. It is how to build a framework where useful experimentation can continue without turning every new capability into an unmanaged public experiment.

How AI can concentrate or redistribute power

AI can concentrate power because it rewards scale. The organizations that control the largest models, the most computing capacity, the most valuable data, and the most widely used distribution channels are often able to improve faster than everyone else. That creates a compounding advantage. A company with deeper pockets can train better systems, offer them at lower prices, attract more users, collect more feedback, and refine the product again. In a market like that, size is not just a measure of success; it becomes a mechanism for making success harder for others to catch.

This is one reason generative AI can feel like a force that pulls activity toward a few large hubs. The technology is expensive to build, expensive to run, and difficult to reproduce from scratch. Even when smaller firms can use the models through an interface or an application programming layer, they may still depend on the infrastructure, rules, and pricing decisions of a handful of providers. That dependence gives platform owners leverage over what gets built, how it is delivered, and who can afford to use it. The power is not only in the model itself, but in the gatekeeping around the model.

Concentration also happens inside organizations. AI can make managers see more, measure more, and intervene more quickly. A system that drafts reports, summarizes performance, flags anomalies, or monitors customer interactions can give leaders a wider field of view than they had before. That can improve coordination, but it can also shift decision-making upward. When information is filtered through dashboards and automated summaries, the people closest to the work may lose some of the discretion they once had. The result can be a more centralized workplace, where the speed of AI is used to tighten oversight rather than broaden autonomy.

At the same time, AI can redistribute power by lowering the cost of capability. A small business that could never hire a full marketing team, legal staff, research assistant, or multilingual support unit may now approximate parts of those functions with a few tools and a small number of people. An individual worker can draft, revise, analyze, and present at a level that once required a larger team. In that sense, AI can act like an amplifier for people and firms that were previously constrained by budget, geography, or access to expertise. The technology does not erase inequality, but it can reduce the distance between those who have large staffs and those who have ingenuity but few resources.

That is why the power effects of AI are rarely one-directional. The same system that helps a small company compete can also make that company more dependent on outside providers. The same tool that gives employees more leverage can also make them easier to compare, rank, and replace. The same model that expands access to knowledge can also be used to shape what knowledge people see first, what options are presented, and what assumptions get built into the interface. AI does not simply hand power to one side or the other. It changes the terms on which power is exercised.

There is also a deeper distributional issue. If AI raises productivity but the gains flow mostly to owners of capital, data, and infrastructure, then the technology can widen inequality even while making society more efficient. If, instead, the gains are shared through lower prices, better services, higher wages for complementary skills, and broader access to tools, then AI can spread value more widely. The economic outcome depends less on the existence of the technology than on who captures the return from it. Research on generative AI and inequality has already raised this concern, noting that the effects on workers and distribution may differ sharply depending on how adoption unfolds [109].

That is why debates over AI are never only about performance. They are about ownership, bargaining power, and institutional design. Who gets access first? Who can afford the best systems? Who sets the rules for use? Who is accountable when the system is wrong? In some settings, AI can reduce the power of intermediaries by letting more people do work directly. In others, it can strengthen intermediaries by giving them better tools to organize attention, labor, and information. The technology is flexible enough to serve both decentralization and control. What determines the outcome is the structure around it: markets, regulation, procurement, labor norms, and the choices made by the institutions deploying it.

What governments and institutions are trying to control

Governments and large institutions are not trying to control AI for one single reason. They are trying to control different parts of it for different reasons: safety, competition, privacy, national security, labor stability, and public trust. That makes the policy landscape look fragmented, but the underlying pattern is consistent. Once a technology becomes capable of influencing speech, decisions, and workflows at scale, institutions begin asking the same basic question: who is responsible when it goes wrong, and who gets to decide how widely it should spread?

One obvious target is harmful use. AI can lower the cost of producing spam, scams, fake identities, manipulated media, and automated harassment. It can also help attackers write more convincing phishing messages, search for weaknesses faster, or adapt harmful content to different audiences. That is why security agencies and policy groups focus on misuse as much as on the models themselves. The concern is not only that a system may be inaccurate, but that it may be put to work in ways that are deliberately deceptive or damaging [6]. In other words, control is partly about reducing the number of people who can use powerful tools to scale harm.

Another target is data. Generative systems depend on vast amounts of text, images, audio, and behavioral information, and that creates pressure from privacy regulators and institutional gatekeepers. Organizations want to know what data went into a model, whether personal or sensitive information was included, whether copyrighted material was used in training, and whether the resulting system can reveal anything it should not. These questions are especially important because AI does not just store data; it can reproduce patterns from data in ways that are hard to trace. So institutions are trying to control not only the output, but the pipeline that produced it.

There is also a growing effort to control deployment inside workplaces, schools, hospitals, and public agencies. Leaders do not want employees or students using powerful tools in ways that expose confidential information, distort records, or create hidden dependencies. That is why many institutions are writing internal rules about approved systems, prohibited uses, human review, and audit trails. The issue is not simply whether AI is useful. It is whether the institution can preserve accountability when the work is partly done by a system that no one fully understands or directly supervises [3]. In practice, governance often means deciding where a machine may assist, where it may advise, and where a human must remain the final decision-maker.

Governments are also trying to control the pace of diffusion. If AI spreads too quickly, policymakers worry that labor markets, education systems, and public services will be forced to absorb the shock before institutions have time to adapt. If it spreads too slowly, they worry about lost innovation, weaker competitiveness, and the concentration of advantage in a few firms or countries. This is why regulation often appears cautious rather than decisive. Officials are trying to avoid both extremes at once. They want enough oversight to prevent obvious harm, but not so much restriction that the technology hardens into a monopoly or migrates to places with looser rules.

That tension is especially visible in the competition between national security and openness. On one side, governments want to keep advanced systems from being used in cyberattacks, fraud, surveillance, or military applications. On the other side, they do not want to block research, entrepreneurship, or broad access to useful tools. The result is a patchwork of controls: export limits on advanced chips, reporting requirements for frontier models, rules for sensitive sectors, and scrutiny of cross-border data flows. The policy goal is not to stop AI entirely. It is to decide which capabilities should be widely available and which should remain under tighter supervision.

Institutions are also trying to control legitimacy. As AI-generated text, images, and audio become easier to produce, trust becomes harder to maintain. A university wants to know whether a student wrote the paper. A news organization wants to know whether a quote is authentic. A bank wants to know whether a customer request is real. A court wants to know whether evidence has been manipulated. That is why attention is shifting toward disclosure, watermarking, provenance tracking, and documentation. These mechanisms are imperfect, but they reflect a broader institutional instinct: if content can be generated cheaply and convincingly, then systems of trust have to become more explicit and more procedural.

What makes all of this difficult is that control is never just technical. It is political, economic, and organizational. A rule that looks reasonable to one group may look like a barrier to innovation to another. A safeguard that protects users may also slow adoption. A requirement that improves accountability may also favor large firms that can afford compliance. This is why the struggle over AI control is really a struggle over standards: who sets them, who has to follow them, and whose interests they are designed to serve. The institutions that shape those standards will influence not only how safe AI becomes, but also how widely its benefits and burdens are distributed.

CHAPTER 9

Chapter 9: Risks, Limits, and the Human Factors That Still Matter

The most important thing to understand about generative AI is not that it fails, but that it fails in ways that can be easy to miss when the output looks polished and the workflow feels smooth. The system may be fast, fluent, and broadly useful, yet still produce results that are incomplete, distorted, or poorly matched to the situation at hand. That is why the risks are not limited to obvious mistakes; they also include the quieter ways a tool can shape judgment, lower scrutiny, or encourage overconfidence in outputs that have not been properly checked.

Common failure modes and why they happen

One common failure mode is hallucination: the system produces something that sounds complete, but is partly invented, outdated, or simply wrong. This happens because the model is optimized to generate the most plausible response, not to verify every statement against a trusted record. In ordinary use, that can look harmless—a wrong date, a misquoted phrase, a fabricated citation—but the problem gets more serious when the output is treated as if it were checked fact. The danger is not only that the model can be wrong. It is that it can be wrong in a way that preserves the shape of confidence. A polished paragraph can hide weak grounding more effectively than a rough draft ever could.

A second failure mode is overgeneralization. These systems are trained on vast mixtures of examples, so they often respond by smoothing differences that matter. A prompt about one industry can receive advice that sounds broadly reasonable but ignores local rules, unusual constraints, or the actual sequence of work. This is one reason AI can be useful for first drafts and dangerous for final judgments. It tends to answer at the level of pattern rather than circumstance. That is especially risky when the task depends on exceptions, edge cases, or tacit knowledge that does not appear clearly in the training data. The model may not be careless; it may simply be applying the wrong kind of generality to a specific problem.

A third failure mode is instruction drift. As prompts get longer, more layered, or more conditional, the system may lose track of what matters most. It may follow the tone request but miss the format, obey the format but ignore a key constraint, or satisfy the last instruction while dropping an earlier one. This is not unusual behavior for a system that is generating text step by step rather than holding a full plan in mind. Users experience it as inconsistency: the output starts well, then wanders, repeats itself, contradicts earlier lines, or quietly abandons the task. The more complex the request, the more likely the model is to approximate the request rather than execute it with precision.

There is also the problem of prompt sensitivity. Small changes in wording can produce noticeably different results, not because the underlying question has changed, but because the model has latched onto a different cue. That makes outcomes feel unstable in a way many users do not expect from software. A manager may ask the same question twice and get two useful but different answers. A student may rephrase a prompt and suddenly receive a response that is more confident, more cautious, or more off target. This variability is part of what makes generative systems powerful, but it also makes them harder to govern.

The tool is not simply retrieving a fixed answer; it is constructing one from context, and context can be fragile.

Another recurring failure mode is fabricated coherence. The model can assemble a response that reads as if it reflects careful reasoning, even when the chain of thought is incomplete or the conclusion does not actually follow. This is especially common when the system is asked to explain, justify, or compare. It may produce a neat structure, a balanced tone, and a persuasive conclusion that gives the impression of analysis. But structure is not the same as rigor. A response can sound like an argument while skipping the hard part of the argument. That matters in business, education, and policy, where the appearance of reasoning can be mistaken for reasoning itself. Research on workplace AI adoption has repeatedly found that implementation is shaped not just by the tool, but by how people adapt their review and oversight practices around it [67].

Some failures come not from the model alone, but from the way people use it. When users treat AI as a shortcut around thinking, they are more likely to accept weak answers, miss errors, or overlook missing context. When organizations deploy it without clear boundaries, the system can drift into tasks it was never meant to handle. When teams rely on it for drafting, sorting, or summarizing, they may stop noticing what has been omitted in the process. The result is a subtle shift in standards: work gets faster, but scrutiny can thin out. That is why the most persistent danger is often not a dramatic mistake. It is a gradual lowering of the threshold for what counts as "good enough."

These failure modes happen because generative AI is not a mind with stable beliefs, situated awareness, or responsibility. It is a pattern engine operating under pressure to produce plausible output quickly. That design makes it flexible and useful, but it also means the system has no built-in sense of when a task is too ambiguous, a claim too important, or a context too sensitive. In practice, the output can look more complete than it is. The human user still has to decide whether the answer is merely fluent or actually fit for purpose. In that sense, the central challenge is not only technical reliability. It is preserving judgment in environments where the machine is very good at sounding like judgment already happened.

Bias, misinformation, and harmful outputs

Bias in generative AI is not always the result of a single bad rule or a deliberately unfair choice. More often, it emerges from the ordinary ingredients that go into the system: the data it learns from, the patterns it is rewarded for reproducing, and the human judgments used to tune it after training. If the underlying material contains stereotypes, imbalances, or gaps, the model can absorb those patterns and reproduce them in new forms. Even when the output looks neutral, it may still reflect uneven assumptions about race, gender, class, geography, language, or profession. Because these systems are so fluent, the bias can be subtle. It may not announce itself as prejudice. It may appear as a default example, a tone choice, a missing perspective, or a recommendation that consistently favors one type of user over another.

This is one reason alignment has become such a central issue in the field. As systems become more capable, the challenge is not only making them more useful, but making them behave in ways that fit human intentions and values [21]. That sounds straightforward until one asks whose intentions, whose values, and in what context. A hiring assistant, a classroom tutor, a customer service bot, and a medical drafting tool all carry different stakes. A model that seems harmless in one setting may be problematic in another because the cost of error is different, the audience is different, and the meaning of "fair" is different. The difficulty is not just technical. It is organizational and social. A company can reduce one kind of bias while unintentionally creating another if it optimizes for speed, politeness, or user satisfaction without checking who is being left out or misrepresented.

Misinformation is closely related, but not identical. Bias often bends the frame through which information is presented. Misinformation can simply be wrong. Generative systems can produce false statements with the same grammatical confidence they use for accurate ones, which makes them especially risky when users assume the output has been verified. A model may invent a citation, merge two separate facts into one, or confidently answer a question it does not truly know how to answer. In practice, that means the problem is not limited to obvious fabrications. It also includes partial truths, outdated claims, and summaries that strip away the context needed to interpret them correctly. The output can look polished enough to pass a quick glance, which is exactly what makes it dangerous.

The risk grows when a system is used as a shortcut for research, drafting, or decision support. If a user asks for a summary of a policy, a legal issue, a scientific finding, or a current event, the model may produce something that sounds coherent even when it is missing key distinctions. That can lead to a second-order problem: people stop checking as carefully because the machine has made the answer feel finished. In other words, misinformation is not only about false content entering the system. It is also about false confidence entering the workflow. Once a fluent answer is on the screen, it can anchor the user's thinking even if the answer is incomplete or wrong.

Harmful outputs are the broadest category because they include more than factual error. They can include insulting language, discriminatory advice, unsafe instructions, sexual content involving minors, encouragement of self-harm, or guidance that helps someone misuse a tool or evade safeguards. Some harms are direct and obvious. Others are indirect. A model that repeatedly treats one group as the norm and another as an exception can reinforce exclusion without ever using abusive language. A system that overproduces cautious disclaimers may frustrate users but still be safer than one that sounds decisive while being wrong. The point is that harm is not measured only by intention. It is measured by impact, and impact depends on how the system is used, by whom, and in what setting.

This is why companies spend so much time on content filters, post-training adjustments, red-teaming, and human review. Those measures do not eliminate the problem, but they can reduce the most serious failures before they reach users. They also reveal an important truth: generative AI is not a self-correcting oracle. It is a probabilistic system that can be steered, constrained, and improved, but never made perfectly safe through one final fix. The challenge is ongoing because the same model can be used for benign drafting in the morning and harmful manipulation by evening. As the OECD's framework for AI classification suggests, the real issue is not just what the system is, but how it is deployed, for what purpose, and under what level of oversight [105].

That is why the most practical response is not blind trust or blanket rejection. It is disciplined use. Users need to know when the system is operating as a helpful first pass and when the stakes require independent verification. Organizations need policies that match the risk of the task, not just the convenience of the tool. And developers need to keep treating bias, misinformation, and harmful outputs as design problems, not edge cases. The more central generative AI becomes to everyday work, the more important it is to remember that fluency is not the same as truth, and confidence is not the same as care.

Security, privacy, and misuse risks

Security risk begins with a simple property of generative systems: they are built to produce convincing output, not to certify truth, identity, or intent. That makes them useful in ordinary work and dangerous in the wrong hands. A model that can draft an email, summarize a policy, or generate code can also be used to impersonate a colleague, polish a scam, or accelerate the search for weaknesses in a system. The same fluency that makes these tools feel helpful can make malicious output feel legitimate. Research on the malicious use of AI has long pointed to this dual-use problem: capabilities that improve productivity can also lower the cost of deception, manipulation, and attack [6].

One of the clearest risks is social engineering at scale. In the past, a convincing phishing attempt often required time, language skill, and a fair amount of manual effort. Generative AI reduces those barriers. It can produce messages that sound natural in different tones, adapt to a target's role, or imitate the style of a real organization. It can also generate many variants quickly, which makes testing and refinement easier for attackers. That does not mean every suspicious message is machine-generated, but it does mean the volume and quality of deceptive content can rise at the same time. The old advice to "look for bad grammar" becomes less useful when the grammar is flawless.

Impersonation is only one part of the problem. Generative systems can also be used to create false documents, synthetic voices, fabricated images, and video that appears credible enough to pass a casual glance. In a business setting, that can mean a fake invoice, a forged approval, or a realistic-looking instruction from someone who seems to have authority. In a political setting, it can mean manufactured statements, fake evidence, or targeted propaganda designed to inflame confusion before anyone has time to verify the source. The threat is not just that false content exists; it is that it can be produced faster than human review can comfortably keep up.

Privacy risk often comes from a different direction. People tend to think of privacy as a matter of what a model knows, but in practice it is also about what users reveal to the model. Employees paste confidential drafts into public tools. Students upload class materials. Consumers share personal details in a moment of convenience because the system appears conversational and safe. Once information leaves the original environment, the user may lose control over how it is stored, reviewed, or reused. Even when a provider has policies intended to limit retention or training use, the basic problem remains: the more a tool is asked to know, the more it can become a repository for sensitive material.

This is especially important because generative systems sit in the middle of many workflows. They are not only outputs; they are also inputs, and sometimes hidden intermediaries. A customer support agent may use one to summarize a complaint. A lawyer may use one to reshape a draft. A manager may use one to condense a meeting note. Each step can expose fragments of data that were never meant to leave their original context. The danger is cumulative. A single prompt may feel harmless, but repeated use can create a trail of confidential details across many sessions, tools, and vendors.

There is also a quieter privacy issue: models can reveal patterns about the data they were trained on or the prompts they have seen. That does not mean every system is leaking private information all the time. It does mean that privacy is not guaranteed simply because the interaction feels ephemeral. As standards and frameworks for AI transparency have noted, users and organizations need clearer visibility into how systems are built, what they retain, and how outputs are generated [35]. Without that visibility, it becomes hard to know whether a tool is merely assisting a task or quietly creating a new data exposure point.

Misuse risk grows when access is broad and controls are weak. A powerful model does not need to be perfect to be harmful; it only needs to be good enough to help someone move faster than they could on their own. That is why organizations increasingly think in terms of permissioning, logging, red-teaming, and escalation paths rather than simple trust. Not every user should be able to send sensitive material to an external system. Not every output should be acted on without review. Not every model should be connected to internal systems, financial actions, or customer-facing channels by default. The more a tool can do, the more carefully it has to be fenced in.

At the same time, security cannot be reduced to blocking access altogether. If people are forced to use AI informally because official tools are too limited or too slow, risk often moves underground instead of disappearing. That is why the practical challenge is not just defense, but governance: choosing where AI is allowed, where it is restricted, what data it can touch, and how its use is monitored. In that sense, the security question is less about whether generative AI is inherently unsafe than about whether institutions can match its speed with policies that are specific enough to matter and flexible enough to survive the next change in capability.

Why human judgment remains central

Generative systems can produce a first pass so quickly and smoothly that it is easy to forget how much work remains after the draft appears. The machine can assemble words, but it cannot decide what matters, what is missing, or what consequences follow if the answer is wrong. That is why human judgment does not become less important as AI improves; it becomes more visible. The better the tool is at generating plausible output, the more the burden shifts to people to evaluate whether that output is appropriate for the situation, the audience, and the stakes. In that sense, AI changes the location of effort more than it eliminates it. It moves labor from composition toward interpretation, from production toward review, and from routine execution toward accountable choice.

This is especially true because many AI outputs are not obviously wrong. They are often polished, coherent, and delivered with the kind of confidence that makes them feel complete. But completeness is not the same as correctness, and fluency is not the same as understanding. A system can produce a recommendation that sounds balanced while quietly omitting a crucial constraint, a legal nuance, or a local fact that changes the decision. Human judgment is the layer that notices when an answer is technically acceptable but practically off target. It is what asks whether a summary leaves out the one detail that matters, whether a draft matches the intended tone, or whether a suggestion is sensible in the real-world context where it will be used.

That kind of judgment is not a vague appeal to intuition. It is a set of human capabilities that AI does not replace well: prioritizing goals, weighing tradeoffs, recognizing exceptions, and understanding responsibility. A model can compare patterns across thousands of examples, but it does not bear the consequences of a mistake. People do. A manager deciding whether to adopt an AI-generated recommendation, a teacher deciding whether a student's work reflects understanding, or a clinician deciding whether a summary is safe to rely on is not simply checking output for errors. They are making a decision under uncertainty, where values, context, and risk all matter. Research on AI alignment emphasizes that as systems become more capable, the challenge is not only technical performance but keeping outputs in line with human intentions and values [21].

That is also why the most important questions around AI are often not "Can it do this?" but "Should it be trusted here?" and "Who is accountable if it fails?" In low-stakes settings, the answer may be to let the system move quickly and accept some imperfection. In higher-stakes settings, the answer may be to slow down, add review, or keep the machine in a supporting role rather than a deciding one. The distinction matters because the same tool can be harmless in one context and damaging in another. A draft email can be corrected easily. A mistaken medical note, payroll error, or compliance summary can create real harm. Human judgment is what calibrates the level of trust to the level of risk.

There is another reason judgment remains central: AI systems are only as useful as the questions they are asked. A weak prompt can produce a weak answer, but a strong prompt still requires the user to know what a strong answer should look like. That means the person using the tool must already understand enough of the subject to evaluate, refine, and redirect it. In practice, AI often rewards people who can define the problem clearly, spot ambiguity, and recognize when the output has drifted. It does not remove expertise; it changes how expertise is expressed. The expert becomes less of a producer of every line and more of an editor, verifier, and strategist.

This shift has organizational consequences as well. Workplaces that adopt AI effectively do not simply hand people a chatbot and assume productivity will follow. They build habits of review, escalation, and accountability around the tool. They decide which tasks can be delegated, which require a second look, and which should remain human-led from the start. Studies of workplace AI implementation show that the results depend heavily on how firms, workers, and managers adapt the surrounding process, not just on the technology itself [67]. That is another way of saying that judgment is not an optional extra. It is part of the system design.

In the end, AI is best understood as a force multiplier for certain kinds of work, not a substitute for responsibility. It can speed up drafting, widen options, and reduce friction. But people still have to decide what counts as good enough, what deserves skepticism, and what should never be outsourced. The more capable the machine becomes, the more important it is to keep a human hand on the wheel—not because humans are always faster or more precise, but because judgment is where meaning, accountability, and context come together.

CHAPTER 10

Chapter 10: How to Adapt and Thrive

Adaptation begins with a clear-eyed view of exposure: not every role, team, or habit is affected in the same way, and the difference matters. Some work will be lightly assisted, some will be reorganized around AI, and some will be pressured to change more quickly than people expect. The point is not to predict every outcome in advance, but to identify where the technology is already touching your decisions, your output, and your standards. From there, the question shifts from fear or enthusiasm to practical judgment: where should you lean in, where should you be cautious, and what kind of learning will actually compound over time?

A practical framework for assessing your AI exposure

A useful way to assess AI exposure is to stop asking whether a job, team, or organization "uses AI" and start asking where generative systems sit in the flow of work. Exposure is not a binary condition. It exists on a spectrum. In some settings, AI is a convenience at the edge of the process: a tool for drafting, summarizing, or brainstorming. In others, it begins to shape the process itself by changing who does the first pass, who verifies the result, and how quickly decisions move. The more a role depends on language, pattern recognition, repeated formatting, and the production of first drafts, the more exposed it tends to be. Research on labor-market impact potential suggests that occupations differ sharply in how much of their task content can be affected by large language models and the software built around them [47].

The first question is simple: which parts of the work are already structured enough for a machine to help? Tasks that have clear inputs, recognizable outputs, and a tolerable amount of variation are the easiest to automate or accelerate. That includes writing routine messages, extracting information from documents, organizing material into a standard format, answering common questions, and generating options from a defined prompt. If a task can be described in a few sentences, repeated many times, and checked after the fact, it is probably exposed. If it depends on tacit knowledge, physical presence, trust, or a high-stakes judgment call, it is usually less exposed, though still not immune. The point is not that AI takes over a whole job at once; it is that it begins by entering the seams between tasks.

The second question is: what happens when the machine is wrong? Exposure rises when a task is not only easy to generate, but also easy to trust too quickly. A draft email that is slightly off is a nuisance. A misread policy, a fabricated citation, or an incorrect recommendation can create real cost. In practice, the riskiest tasks are often the ones where AI output looks polished enough to discourage scrutiny. That is why the human role shifts from producing every word to setting standards, checking edge cases, and deciding when a draft is good enough to move forward. In organizational settings, this changes job design as much as it changes productivity: workers spend less time making the first version and more time reviewing, correcting, and coordinating [3].

A third question is whether AI changes the economics of the work. Even when a tool does not fully automate a task, it can reduce the time and cost required to complete it. That matters because small reductions compound. If a team can produce proposals, reports, support replies, or research summaries faster, the bottleneck may shift from drafting to approval, from search to judgment, or from production to distribution. A role is therefore more exposed when speed and volume are central to its value. By contrast, work that is valued for deep relationships, specialized accountability, or bespoke judgment may be altered, but not easily replaced. Exposure is highest where output is plentiful, standardized, and measured by throughput rather than by unique human presence.

It also helps to distinguish between task exposure and career exposure. A person can be highly exposed at the task level and still have a durable career if the surrounding work is hard to automate. For example, a manager may use AI to draft communications, summarize meetings, or prepare talking points, yet still be responsible for motivating people, resolving conflict, and making tradeoffs under uncertainty. The reverse is also true: a role may look secure because it contains some human-facing elements, but if its core value comes from repetitive knowledge work, it may be more vulnerable than it first appears. This is why broad job titles can be misleading. What matters is the bundle of activities inside the job, not the label on the business card.

A practical exposure assessment asks four questions in order. First, how much of this work is text, pattern, or repetition? Second, how often is a first draft or first answer enough to move the process forward? Third, how much checking is required before the output can be trusted? Fourth, if the work became faster and cheaper, would the organization change how much of it it buys, assigns, or expects? If the answer to the first two is yes and the answer to the third is manageable, exposure is likely high. If the work is difficult to specify, difficult to verify, or deeply tied to human trust, exposure is lower. This framework is not meant to predict exact outcomes. It is meant to show where pressure is already building.

There is one more layer that often gets overlooked: institutional readiness. Two people can perform the same role and face very different exposure depending on the culture around them. In one organization, AI may be welcomed as a drafting aid with clear review rules. In another, it may be adopted informally, without standards, creating confusion about quality and responsibility. Higher education is already seeing this kind of uneven adoption, with institutions forced to rethink assessment, policy, and student support as generative tools become normal parts of the environment [86]. The same pattern appears in business and public-sector settings. Exposure is not only about the technology itself; it is also about whether the surrounding system knows how to absorb it.

For individuals, the most revealing test is often personal: if a capable tool could do the first 60 percent of this task, what would remain uniquely mine? If the answer is mostly formatting, searching, and rewriting, exposure is substantial. If the answer is diagnosis, negotiation, accountability, or original judgment, exposure is lower, though the support work around it may still change. For teams, the question becomes: which tasks should be accelerated, which should be re-designed, and which should be protected from premature automation? That distinction matters because the goal is not to avoid exposure altogether. It is to know where it sits, how fast it is moving, and which parts of the work deserve a human checkpoint before the machine's speed becomes the organization's default.

How to experiment safely and learn quickly

The safest way to learn AI is to treat it like a new workplace tool, not a toy and not a trusted colleague. That means starting with low-stakes tasks where errors are annoying rather than costly: rewriting a paragraph, drafting a routine email, summarizing notes, outlining a presentation, or generating a list of options you will later review yourself. The point of those early experiments is not to get perfect output. It is to learn the system's habits—how it responds to vague prompts, where it becomes overly confident, how much context it needs, and what kinds of tasks it handles well enough to save time. In organizations, this kind of controlled experimentation is increasingly important because AI is showing up across many kinds of work, but the effects depend heavily on how it is introduced into actual routines [3].

A good experiment begins with a clear boundary. Decide in advance what the tool is allowed to touch and what it is not. For example, you might use AI on public-facing material that is already in draft form, but not on confidential client data, personal records, or anything that carries legal, medical, or financial consequences. You might let it propose wording, but not make the final decision. You might ask it to generate alternatives, but not to supply facts unless you can verify them elsewhere. These limits are not signs of fear; they are what make learning possible. When the stakes are controlled, you can observe the tool more carefully and build a realistic sense of where it belongs in your workflow.

The fastest learners do not ask, "Can this tool do my job?" They ask, "Which part of my job is easiest to test?" That shift matters because AI adoption is rarely all-or-nothing. It usually begins with a single task, then expands if the first trial is useful. A manager might test it on meeting summaries before using it for project briefs. A student might use it to explain a concept before relying on it to help structure an essay. A marketer might compare machine-generated subject lines against their own. Each test should have a simple standard: save time, improve clarity, generate options, or reduce repetitive effort. If the tool does none of those things reliably, it may still be interesting, but it is not yet useful in that setting.

It also helps to test the system in pairs: one prompt that is loose and one that is specific. Loose prompts reveal how the model behaves when it has to infer too much. Specific prompts reveal whether better instructions produce better results. If the output improves dramatically when you add context, examples, audience, and constraints, then the lesson is not that the system is magically smart; it is that prompting is part of the work. If the output remains shallow or off target even after careful guidance, that is valuable information too. It tells you the task may be poorly suited to the tool, or that the tool should remain a first-pass assistant rather than a central part of the process.

Verification should be built into the experiment from the start. A useful habit is to compare the AI's output against a trusted source, a human draft, or your own knowledge before you decide whether it is good enough. This is especially important because fluent output can disguise weak reasoning or invented details. A system may sound polished while still being wrong in subtle ways. The danger is not only obvious factual errors; it is the gradual erosion of scrutiny when the text looks professional enough to pass at a glance. Research on alignment and misuse makes clear that as systems become more capable, the importance of checking behavior against human intent and safety constraints only grows [21]. In practice, that means treating the first answer as a draft, not a verdict.

Learning quickly also means keeping notes. Most people forget the exact prompt that worked, the type of task that failed, or the point where the model became unreliable. A simple log—what you asked, what came back, what you changed, and whether the result was useful—turns scattered experimentation into accumulated knowledge. Over time, that record tells you more than general commentary about AI ever could, because it reflects your own use case. It shows where the tool helps you move faster, where it creates extra cleanup, and where human judgment still dominates. That is the real advantage of safe experimentation: it turns uncertainty into evidence.

As the experiments get more useful, resist the temptation to expand them everywhere at once. The goal is not to make AI the default answer to every problem. The goal is to learn where it adds leverage without weakening quality, accountability, or trust. In some settings, the right move will be to use it constantly. In others, the right move will be to keep it at the edge of the process or leave it out entirely. The organizations and individuals that adapt best are usually not the ones that adopt fastest in a blind rush. They are the ones that test carefully, learn quickly, and keep the human standard in place while the machine does the parts it can do well.

Skills that compound in an AI-driven world

The skills that compound in an AI-driven world are not the same skills that used to matter most in a world of scarce drafting, scarce analysis, and scarce first attempts. When software can produce a passable outline, a polished email, or a quick summary almost instantly, the advantage shifts away from sheer output and toward the abilities that improve every time they are used. These are the skills that help a person choose the right problem, frame it clearly, test the machine's result, and turn an adequate draft into a reliable decision or a better finished product.

One of the most important of these is problem definition. AI is highly responsive to the shape of the prompt, which means that people who can specify the goal, audience, constraints, and desired standard of quality get far better results than people who ask vaguely for "help." In practice, that means learning to translate a messy objective into something the system can work with: What is the task? What does success look like? What should be excluded? What tone or format is required? The better a person becomes at defining the problem, the more useful the machine becomes as a force multiplier.

Closely related is judgment, especially the judgment to distinguish between a fluent answer and a correct one. Generative systems can produce convincing prose even when they are wrong, incomplete, or poorly matched to context. That makes evaluation a compounding skill because every use of AI creates another opportunity to practice noticing weak assumptions, missing evidence, and overconfident language. People who get better at checking claims, comparing alternatives, and recognizing when something "sounds right" but is not actually right will gain an advantage that does not depend on any single tool. Their standards improve, and so does the quality of everything they touch.

Taste also matters more than it used to. Taste is not just aesthetic preference; it is the ability to recognize what is good enough, what is promising, what is off, and what deserves refinement. In an AI-rich environment, a lot of work arrives as options. The machine can generate ten versions of a headline, five possible approaches to a presentation, or several rewrites of a paragraph. The scarce skill is no longer producing the first version. It is selecting, editing, and combining the versions that best fit the purpose. Over time, people with strong taste build a sharper sense of quality, and that sense helps them use AI without becoming dependent on whatever it happens to generate first.

Another compounding skill is domain knowledge. The more a person knows about a field, the more effectively they can direct AI and catch its mistakes. A novice may be impressed by a plausible answer; an expert is more likely to see where the answer is thin, generic, outdated, or subtly misleading. This is why AI does not erase the value of expertise. In many cases, it increases it. The system can speed up routine work, but it still needs a human who understands the deeper structure of the subject, the practical constraints, and the real-world consequences of getting the answer wrong. The stronger the domain knowledge, the more leverage the person gets from the tool.

There is also a premium on communication in the broad sense: writing clearly, asking precise questions, explaining tradeoffs, and aligning people around a decision. A great deal of work in organizations is not purely technical; it is coordination. AI can assist with drafts and summaries, but it does not remove the need to persuade, clarify, negotiate, and make meaning across different audiences. In fact, because AI makes the production of text cheaper, the ability to communicate with purpose becomes more valuable, not less. The people who can turn a rough machine-generated draft into something that actually moves a project forward will increasingly stand out.

Workflow design is another skill that compounds because it changes how all the other skills are used. Someone who knows how to break a task into steps, identify where AI fits, and insert human review at the right moments can produce far more value than someone who simply uses the tool ad hoc. This is where experimentation becomes a serious professional habit: trying different prompts, comparing outputs, measuring time saved, and noticing where a process still breaks down. Research on organizational AI use shows that the impact is not only about the tool itself, but about how it reshapes work design, collaboration, and employee experience [3]. People who learn to redesign their own work are not just using AI better; they are building a transferable capability.

Finally, the most durable compounding skill may be learning speed. AI changes quickly enough that specific tool knowledge ages fast, but the ability to adapt does not. People who stay curious, test new methods, and update their habits without waiting for a formal mandate will keep accumulating advantage. They will also be less likely to freeze when a new system appears or an old process disappears. In an environment where the tools keep changing, the real edge belongs to those who can keep learning while working, and keep working while learning.

Building resilience, flexibility, and long-term advantage

Resilience in an AI-rich environment does not mean resisting the technology or trying to stay untouched by it. It means building a way of working that can absorb change without losing direction. The organizations and individuals most likely to do well are not the ones with the most polished first adoption story. They are the ones that can keep moving when the tools change, the interfaces shift, and the rules of use get rewritten. That starts with a simple recognition: AI is not a one-time upgrade. It is a moving layer of capability that will keep altering how tasks are done, how decisions are made, and how value is created.

That is why flexibility matters as much as efficiency. A workflow that is optimized too tightly around one model, one vendor, or one prompt pattern can become fragile the moment the underlying system changes. By contrast, a flexible workflow keeps the human logic visible. It separates the goal from the tool, the judgment from the draft, and the standard from the mechanism used to meet it. If a team knows exactly what it is trying to produce, what quality looks like, and where review must happen, it can swap tools without rebuilding its entire process. The same principle applies to individual work. A person who depends on AI to produce a finished result without understanding the steps in between is building speed on top of uncertainty.

Long-term advantage comes from using AI to increase option value, not just short-term output. The obvious use of generative systems is to do familiar work faster: draft the memo, summarize the meeting, generate the slide deck, sort the inbox. Those gains matter, but they are only the first layer. The deeper advantage appears when AI helps people test more possibilities, compare more alternatives, and move from idea to experiment with less friction. Research on human and generative AI interaction suggests that the strongest results often come from collaborative decision-making rather than from handing the entire decision over to the machine [49]. In other words, the payoff is not only speed. It is better exploration.

That changes what it means to be valuable. In the past, advantage often came from being the person who could produce more than others: more pages, more reports, more analysis, more drafts. In an AI-enabled setting, that edge narrows quickly. What compounds instead is the ability to define problems clearly, set standards, evaluate output, and connect machine-generated material to real-world constraints. People who can do that well become harder to replace because they are not merely completing tasks. They are shaping the work itself. They know when to use AI for first-pass generation, when to ask for alternatives, when to slow down, and when to insist on human review.

Resilience also depends on keeping skills broad enough to travel across roles and tools. The more narrowly a person's value is tied to one specific software habit, the more vulnerable that value becomes when the habit changes. Broad skills such as writing clearly, reasoning about tradeoffs, understanding customers, managing projects, and spotting weak assumptions remain useful even as the surrounding technology evolves. These are not “soft” skills in the weak sense. They are transfer skills. They make it easier to learn new systems, supervise automated output, and move into adjacent work when a job changes shape. In a period of rapid digital transformation, that kind of portability is a major asset [22].

For organizations, long-term advantage often comes from building an environment where people can experiment without losing control. That means creating room for small tests, shared standards, and clear rules about where AI can and cannot be used. It also means avoiding the trap of measuring success only by time saved. A faster process that produces more errors, more confusion, or more dependency is not resilient. A better test is whether the team can still perform well when the tool fails, when the model output is weak, or when a task needs to be handed back to human judgment. The best systems do not hide the human role; they make it more deliberate.

There is also a strategic advantage in learning to work with uncertainty instead of waiting for certainty. AI capabilities will keep improving, but they will not arrive in a neat sequence that allows everyone to plan perfectly. New features will appear, some will be overhyped, and others will become unexpectedly useful. The practical response is not to predict every turn. It is to build habits that make change less costly: document what works, keep review steps visible, train people to evaluate outputs critically, and preserve enough flexibility to adjust when the next wave arrives. In that sense, resilience is not a defensive posture. It is a way of staying capable while the ground keeps moving.

Citations

The following sources were referenced in the preceding chapters. Each entry links back to the inline reference in the text. All sources were verified against the OpenAlex academic database at the time of generation.

1. Leonardo Banh, Gero Strobel (2023). Generative artificial intelligence. https://doi.org/10.1007/s12525-023-00680-1

2. Shanaka Kristombu Baduge, Sadeep Thilakarathna, Jude Shalitha Perera et al. (2022). Artificial intelligence and smart vision for building and construction 4.0: Machine and deep learning methods and applications. https://doi.org/10.1016/j.autcon.2022.104440

3. Sarah Bankins, Anna Carmella Ocampo, Mauricio Marrone et al. (2023). A multilevel review of artificial intelligence in organizations: Implications for organizational behavior research and practice. https://doi.org/10.1002/job.2735

4. Dominik K. Kanbach, Louisa Heiduk, Georg Blueher et al. (2023). The GenAI is out of the bottle: generative artificial intelligence from a business model innovation perspective. https://doi.org/10.1007/s11846-023-00696-z

5. Marcello M. Mariani, Rodrigo Perez-Vega, Jochen Wirtz (2021). AI in marketing, consumer research and psychology: A systematic literature review and research agenda. https://doi.org/10.1002/mar.21619

6. Miles Brundage, Shahar Avin, Jack Clark et al. (2018). The malicious use of artificial intelligence: Forecasting, prevention, and mitigation. https://doi.org/10.17863/cam.22520

7. Victoria Jackson, Bogdan Vasilescu, Daniel Russo et al. (2024). The Impact of Generative AI on Creativity in Software Development: A Research Agenda. https://doi.org/10.1145/3708523

8. Frank M. Fossen, Trevor McLemore, Alina Sorgner (2024). Artificial Intelligence and Entrepreneurship. https://doi.org/10.2139/ssrn.4863772

9. Waldemar Karwowski, Gavriel Salvendy, Laura A. Albert et al. (2025). Grand challenges in industrial and systems engineering. https://doi.org/10.1080/00207543.2024.2432463

10. Gokul Yenduri, M. Ramalingam, Чурашов А.Г. et al. (2023). Generative Pre-trained Transformer: A Comprehensive Review on Enabling Technologies, Potential Applications, Emerging Challenges, and Future Directions. https://doi.org/10.48550/arxiv.2305.10435

11. Felipe A. Csaszar, Michael G. Jacobides, Peter Zemsky (2025). The Effects of Artificial Intelligence on Management Education. https://doi.org/10.2139/ssrn.5325783

12. Benjamin Schneider, Hillary Vipond (2023). The Past and Future of Work: How History Can Inform the Age of Automation. https://doi.org/10.2139/ssrn.4643947

13. Stefan Feuerriegel, Jochen Hartmann, Christian Janiesch et al. (2023). Generative AI. https://doi.org/10.1007/s12599-023-00834-7

14. Nicholas G. Otis, Rowan Philip Clarke, Solène Delecourt et al. (2023). The Uneven Impact of Generative AI on Entrepreneurial Performance. https://doi.org/10.31219/osf.io/hdjpk

15. Francesco Filippucci, Péter Gál, Cecilia Jona-Lasinio et al. (2024). The impact of Artificial Intelligence on productivity, distribution and growth. https://doi.org/10.1787/8d900037-en

16. Yee Zhing Liew, Andrew Huey Ping Tan, Eng Hwa Yap et al. (2024). Systems Thinking on Artificial Intelligence Integration into Higher Education: Causal Loops. https://doi.org/10.5772/intechopen.1008246

17. Matti Mäkelin (2019). Digital transformation as expanding strategy and structure. https://openalex.org/W2966229646

18. James Hutson (2024). Rethinking Plagiarism in the Era of Generative AI. https://doi.org/10.54963/jic.v4i1.220

19. B. A. Adewale, Vincent Onyedikachi Ene, Babatunde Fatai Ogunbayo et al. (2024). A Systematic Review of the Applications of AI in a Sustainable Building's Lifecycle. https://doi.org/10.3390/buildings14072137

20. Elsa Delgado-Sánchez, Reyes Calderón, Francisco Herrera (2025). Artificial Intelligence Adoption in SMEs: Survey Based on TOE–DOI Framework, Primary Methodology and Challenges. https://doi.org/10.3390/app15126465

21. Jiaming Ji, Tianyi Qiu, Boyuan Chen et al. (2023). AI Alignment: A Comprehensive Survey. https://doi.org/10.48550/arxiv.2310.19852

22. Justin Paul, Akiko Ueno, Charles Dennis et al. (2024). Digital transformation: A multidisciplinary perspective and future research agenda. https://doi.org/10.1111/ijcs.13015

23. Dimple Patil, Nitin Liladhar Rane, Jayesh Rane et al. (2024). Artificial intelligence and generative AI, such as ChatGPT, in transportation: Applications, technologies, challenges, and ethical considerations. https://doi.org/10.70593/978-81-981367-4-9_6

24. Radosław Wolniak, Kinga Stecuła, Barış Aydın (2024). Digital Transformation of Grocery In-Store Shopping-Scanners, Artificial Intelligence, Augmented Reality and Beyond: A Review. https://doi.org/10.3390/foods13182948

25. OECD (2023). AI language models. https://doi.org/10.1787/13d38f92-en

26. Srinivasa Rao Challa (2023). Artificial Intelligence and Big Data in Finance: Enhancing Investment Strategies and Client Insights in Wealth Management. https://doi.org/10.21275/sr231215165201

27. Andrei Kucharavy, Z. M. Schillaci, Loïc Maréchal et al. (2023). Fundamentals of Generative Large Language Models and Perspectives in Cyber-Defense. https://doi.org/10.48550/arxiv.2303.12132

28. Bhaskar Mitra, Henriette Cramer, Olya Gurevich (2024). Socio-technical Implications of Generative Artificial Intelligence for Information Access. https://doi.org/10.48550/arxiv.2405.11612

29. Xiangyu Li, Yuqing Fan, Shenghui Cheng (2023). AIGC In China: Current Developments And Future Outlook. https://doi.org/10.48550/arxiv.2308.08451

30. Heidi Heimberger, Djerdj Horvat, Frank Schultmann (2024). Exploring the factors driving AI adoption in production: a systematic literature review and future research agenda. https://doi.org/10.1007/s10799-024-00436-z

31. Aditya Pathak, Radhika Theagarajan, Muhammad Miftakhur Rizqi et al. (2025). AI-enabled drug and molecular discovery: computational methods, platforms, and translational horizons. https://doi.org/10.1007/s44345-025-00037-5

32. Daniel Russo (2024). Navigating the Complexity of Generative AI Adoption in Software Engineering. https://doi.org/10.1145/3652154

33. Wayne F. Cascio, Ramiro Montealegre (2016). How Technology Is Changing Work and Organizations. https://doi.org/10.1146/annurev-orgpsych-041015-062352

34. Justyna Dąbrowska, Argyro Almpanopoulou, Alexander Brem et al. (2022). Digital transformation, for better or worse: a critical multi-level research agenda. https://doi.org/10.1111/radm.12531

35. Brady Lund, Zeynep Orhan, Nishith Reddy Mannuru et al. (2025). Standards, frameworks, and legislation for artificial intelligence (AI) transparency. https://doi.org/10.1007/s43681-025-00661-4

36. Yoshija Walter (2024). Managing the race to the moon: Global policy and governance in Artificial Intelligence regulation—A contem-

porary overview and an analysis of socioeconomic consequences. https://doi.org/10.1007/s44163-024-00109-4

37. Mariarosaria Comunale (2024). The Economic Impacts and the Regulation of AI: A Review of the Academic Literature and Policy Actions. https://doi.org/10.5089/9798400268588.001

38. Nisreen Ameen, Shlomo Y. Tarba, Jun-Hwa Cheah et al. (2024). Coupling Artificial Intelligence Capability and Strategic Agility for Enhanced Product and Service Creativity. https://doi.org/10.1111/1467-8551.12797

39. Lynn S. Aaron, Santina Abbate, Nicola Marae Allain et al. (2024). Optimizing AI in Higher Education. https://doi.org/10.2307/jj.20522984

40. Rosa Fioravante, Antonino Vaccaro (2024). Personalism in Generative AI Deployment: Deciding Ethically When Human Creative Expression is at Stake. https://doi.org/10.1007/s41463-024-00193-9

41. Paulo Carv�ão, Slavina Ancheva, Yam Atir et al. (2025). Governance at a Crossroads: Artificial Intelligence and the Future of Innovation in America. https://doi.org/10.2139/ssrn.5131048

42. Kristofer Erickson (2024). AI and work in the creative industries: digital continuity or discontinuity?. https://doi.org/10.1080/17510694.2024.2421135

43. Valerio Capraro, Austin Lentsch, Daron Acemoğlu et al. (2023). The impact of generative artificial intelligence on socioeconomic inequalities and policy making. https://doi.org/10.31234/osf.io/6fd2y

44. Ali B. Mahmoud, V Kumar, Stavroula Spyropoulou (2025). Identifying the Public's Beliefs About Generative Artificial Intelligence: A Big Data Approach. https://doi.org/10.1109/tem.2025.3534088

45. Md Ferdous Alam, Austin Lentsch, Nomi Yu et al. (2024). From Automation to Augmentation: Redefining Engineering Design and Man-

ufacturing in the Age of NextGen-AI. https://doi.org/10.21428/e4baed-d9.e39b392d

46. Nicolas Friederici, Michel Njeri Wahome, Mark Graham (2020). Digital Entrepreneurship in Africa. https://doi.org/10.7551/mitpress/12453.001.0001

47. Tyna Eloundou, Sam Manning, Pamela Mishkin et al. (2023). GPTs are GPTs: An Early Look at the Labor Market Impact Potential of Large Language Models. https://doi.org/10.48550/arxiv.2303.10130

48. Roberto Gozalo-Brizuela, Eduardo Eduardo Garrido Merchan (2024). A Survey of Generative AI Applications. https://doi.org/10.3844/jcssp.2024.801.818

49. Xinyue Hao, Emrah Demir, Daniel Eyers (2024). Exploring collaborative decision-making: A quasi-experimental study of human and Generative AI interaction. https://doi.org/10.1016/j.techsoc.2024.102662

50. Ali A. Guenduez, Tobias Mettler (2022). Strategically constructed narratives on artificial intelligence: What stories are told in governmental artificial intelligence policies?. https://doi.org/10.1016/j.giq.2022.101719

51. Hind Benbya, Franz Strich, Toomas Tamm (2024). Navigating Generative Artificial Intelligence Promises and Perils for Knowledge and Creative Work. https://doi.org/10.17705/1jais.00861

52. Zarif Bin Akhtar (2024). Unveiling the evolution of generative AI (GAI): a comprehensive and investigative analysis toward LLM models (2021–2024) and beyond. https://doi.org/10.1186/s43067-024-00145-1

53. Vanshika Vats, Marzia Binta Nizam, Minghao Liu et al. (2024). A Survey on Human-AI Collaboration with Large Foundation Models. https://doi.org/10.48550/arxiv.2403.04931

54. Dave Mbiazi, Meghana Bhange, Maryam Babaei et al. (2023). Survey on AI Ethics: A Socio-technical Perspective. https://doi.org/10.48550/arxiv.2311.17228

55. Emmanuel Alejandro Merchán-Cruz, Ioseb Gabelaia, Mihails Savrasovs et al. (2025). Trust by Design: An Ethical Framework for Collaborative Intelligence Systems in Industry 5.0. https://doi.org/10.3390/electronics14101952

56. Muyanja-Ssenyonga Jameaba (2024). Digitalization, Emerging Technologies, and Financial Stability: Challenges and Opportunities for the Indonesian Banking Sector and Beyond. https://doi.org/10.2139/ssrn.4808469

57. Brent Winslow, Özlem Özmen Garibay, Tesh Goyal et al. (2026). Revisiting the Six Human-Centered Artificial Intelligence Grand Challenges in the Age of Generative AI. https://doi.org/10.1080/10447318.2026.2641703

58. Yujie Cao, Mohammad Azhan Abdul Aziz, Wan Nur Rukiah Mohd Arshard (2023). University students' perspectives on Artificial Intelligence. https://doi.org/10.46661/ijeri.8429

59. Igor Calzada, Géza Németh, Mohammed Salah Al-Radhi (2025). Trustworthy AI for Whom? GenAI Detection Techniques of Trust Through Decentralized Web3 Ecosystems. https://doi.org/10.3390/bdcc9030062

60. Marina Tcharnetsky, Florian Vogt (2023). An Artificial Intelligence Cycle Model Against the Shortage of Skilled Professionals - An AI-based Holistic Solution Approach for Human Resources. https://doi.org/10.57017/jaes.v18.2(80).05

61. Shapira, Philip; id_orcid 0000-0003-2488-5985, Youtie, Jan (2017). The next production revolution and institutions for technology diffusion. https://doi.org/10.1787/9789264271036-11-en

62. Michael J. Salvo, John T. Sherrill (2025). Artificial Infrastructures. https://doi.org/10.37514/pra-b.2025.2654

63. Victor Faessel, Richard Falk, Michael Curtin (2019). On Public Imagination. https://doi.org/10.4324/9780429343599

64. Mauro Cazzaniga (2024). Gen-AI. https://doi.org/10.5089/9798400262548.006

65. Aras Yolusever (2025). AI AND AUTOMATION: RESHAPING THE LABOR MARKET. https://doi.org/10.70754/biibfd.1594580

66. Zhongju Li, Yu Chen (2025). Does Artificial Intelligence Promote Firms' Green Technological Innovation?. https://doi.org/10.3390/su17114900

67. Milanez, Anna (2023). The Impact of AI on the Workplace: Evidence from OECD Case Studies of AI Implementation. https://doi.org/10.1787/2247ce58-en

68. Anders Humlum, Emilie Vestergaard (2025). Still Waters, Rapid Currents: Early Labor Market Transformation under Generative AI. https://doi.org/10.3386/w33777

69. Paweł Gmyrek, Janine Berg, Karol Kamiński et al. (2025). Generative AI and jobs. https://doi.org/10.54394/hetp0387

70. David Kerr, Katherine Taken Smith, L. Murphy Smith et al. (2025). A Review of AI and Its Impact on Management Accounting and Society. https://doi.org/10.3390/jrfm18060340

71. World Bank (2020). Artificial Intelligence in the Public Sector. https://doi.org/10.1596/35317

72. Akram Hakiri, Aniruddha Gokhale, Sadok Ben Yahia et al. (2024). A comprehensive survey on digital twin for future networks and emerging Internet of Things industry. https://doi.org/10.1016/j.comnet.2024.110350

73. Anika Jahan Mou (2025). MARTECH STACK ADOPTION IN SMES: A REVIEW OF AUTOMATION, CRM, AND AI INTEGRATION. https://doi.org/10.63125/y8j1zh51

74. Jianxin Jiao, Sesh Commuri, Jitesh H. Panchal et al. (2021). Design Engineering in the Age of Industry 4.0. https://doi.org/10.1115/1.4051041

75. Ahmed Farouk Kineber, Atul Kumar Singh, Abdulwahed Fazeli et al. (2023). Modelling the relationship between digital twins implementation barriers and sustainability pillars: Insights from building and construction sector. https://doi.org/10.1016/j.scs.2023.104930

76. Jiayuan Chen, You Shi (2024). Generative AI over Mobile Networks for Human Digital Twin in Human-Centric Applications: A Comprehensive Survey. https://doi.org/10.36227/techrxiv.172349525.50239637/v1

77. Muhammad Salar Khan, Hamza Umer, Farhana Faruqe (2024). Artificial intelligence for low income countries. https://doi.org/10.1057/s41599-024-03947-w

78. Patrizia Gazzola, Enrica Pavione, Rainer Hillebrand et al. (2025). The Circular Economy and the Role of Technology in the Fashion Industry: A Comparison of Empirical Evidence. https://doi.org/10.3390/su17073104

79. Kenneth B. Tingey (2025). AI Comments: Leveraging the Global Knowledge Corpus, One Way or Another. https://doi.org/10.62477/jkmp.v25i4.538

80. Unknown author (2024). Technics. https://openalex.org/W7137443949

81. Baer, Nicholas 1985-, van den Oever, Annie (2024). Technics. https://doi.org/10.1515/9789048564569

82. Warren Neidich (2019). The Glossary of Cognitive Activism (For a Not So Distant Future). https://doi.org/10.17613/q57na-g5c77

83. Akriti Taneja, Gayathri Nair, Manisha Joshi et al. (2023). Artificial Intelligence: Implications for the Agri-Food Sector. https://doi.org/10.3390/agronomy13051397

84. Morteza Ghobakhloo, Masood Fathi, Mohammad Iranmanesh et al. (2024). Generative artificial intelligence in manufacturing: opportunities for actualizing Industry 5.0 sustainability goals. https://doi.org/10.1108/jmtm-12-2023-0530

85. Clare Baek, Tamara Tate, Mark Warschauer (2024). "ChatGPT seems too good to be true": College students' use and perceptions of generative AI. https://doi.org/10.1016/j.caeai.2024.100294

86. Laurie Hughes, Tegwen Malik, Sandra Dettmer et al. (2025). Reimagining Higher Education: Navigating the Challenges of Generative AI Adoption. https://doi.org/10.1007/s10796-025-10582-6

87. James Hutson (2024). Rethinking Plagiarism in the Era of Generative AI. https://doi.org/10.54963/jic.v3i2.220

88. Adil S. Al-Busaidi, Raghu Raman, Raghu Raman et al. (2024). Redefining boundaries in innovation and knowledge domains: Investigating the impact of generative artificial intelligence on copyright and intellectual property rights. https://doi.org/10.1016/j.jik.2024.100630

89. Cristo León, James Lipuma, Xavier Oviedo-Torres (2025). Artificial intelligence in STEM education: a transdisciplinary framework for engagement and innovation. https://doi.org/10.3389/feduc.2025.1619888

90. Allison Woodruff, Renee Shelby, Patrick Gage Kelley et al. (2023). How Knowledge Workers Think Generative AI Will (Not) Transform Their Industries. https://doi.org/10.48550/arxiv.2310.06778

91. Peter Bednár, Christine Welch (2019). Socio-Technical Perspectives on Smart Working: Creating Meaningful and Sustainable Systems. https://doi.org/10.1007/s10796-019-09921-1

92. Yogesh K. Dwivedi, Anuj Sharma, Nripendra P. Rana et al. (2023). Evolution of artificial intelligence research in Technological Forecasting and Social Change: Research topics, trends, and future directions. https://doi.org/10.1016/j.techfore.2023.122579

93. Fei Dou, Jin Ye, Yuan Geng et al. (2023). Towards Artificial General Intelligence (AGI) in the Internet of Things (IoT): Opportunities and Challenges. https://doi.org/10.48550/arxiv.2309.07438

94. Antonius Setyadi, Suharno Pawirosumarto, Alana Damaris (2025). Rethinking Sustainable Operations: A Multi-Level Integration of Circularity, Localization, and Digital Resilience in Manufacturing Systems. https://doi.org/10.3390/su17156929

95. Chiara Panaro (2025). Generative AI and strategic decision-making: cognitive shifts, collaboration and organizational change – cognitive convergence in artificial intelligence supported innovation. https://openalex.org/W7162266628

96. Francesca Lannace (2026). Offloading thought: how generative artificial intelligence reshapes ownership and responsibility. https://openalex.org/W7162272454

97. Sang-Woo Oh, Jaemin Jung (2025). Harmonizing Traditional Journalistic Values With Emerging AI Technologies: A Systematic Review of Journalists' Perception. https://doi.org/10.17645/mac.9495

98. Leslie Browning-Samoni (2024). AI and fashion: Student perspectives on the application and ethical use of various forms of Generative Artificial Intelligence (GAI) in a fashion context. https://doi.org/10.31274/td-20240617-32

99. Roi Alfassi, Angelora Cooper, Zoe Mitchell et al. (2025). Fanfiction in the Age of AI: Community Perspectives on Creativity, Authenticity and Adoption. https://doi.org/10.1080/10447318.2025.2531272

100. Segun Kehinde (2025). AI in Everything, and Everything in AI: A Review of the Ubiquitous Role of Artificial Intelligence in Shaping the Next Technological Epoch. https://doi.org/10.69996/jcai.2025024

101. Ritu Raj, Rajesh Chandwani (2025). Navigating "AI-Powered Immersiveness" in Healthcare Delivery: A Case of Indian Doctors. https://doi.org/10.17705/1cais.05545

102. Venetia Brown, Retno Larasati, Joseph Kwarteng et al. (2025). Understanding AI and power: situated perspectives from Global North and South practitioners. https://doi.org/10.1007/s00146-025-02731-x

103. Cristina Alaimo, Jannis Kallinikos (2024). Data Rules. https://doi.org/10.7551/mitpress/11751.001.0001

104. Petter Törnberg, Justus Uitermark (2025). Seeing Like a Platform. https://doi.org/10.4324/9781003326861

105. OECD (2022). OECD Framework for the Classification of AI systems. https://doi.org/10.1787/cb6d9eca-en

106. Dominika Kaczorowska–Spychalska, Nina Kotula, Grzegorz Mazurek et al. (2024). Generative AI as source of change of knowledge management paradigm. https://doi.org/10.14254/1795-6889.2024.20-1.7

107. Francesco Schiavone, Maria Cristina Pietronudo, Annamaria Sabetta et al. (2022). Designing AI implications in the venture creation process. https://doi.org/10.1108/ijebr-06-2021-0483

108. Joakim Laine, Matti Minkkinen, Matti Mäntymäki (2025). Understanding the Ethics of Generative AI: Established and New Ethical Principles. https://doi.org/10.17705/1cais.05601

109. Nathan Wilmers (2024). Generative AI and the Future of Inequality. https://doi.org/10.21428/e4baedd9.777b7123

110. J. Gonzales (2023). Implications of AI innovation on economic growth: a panel data study. https://doi.org/10.1186/s40008-023-00307-w

111. Paolo Bory, Simone Natale, Christian Katzenbach (2024). Strong and weak AI narratives: an analytical framework. https://doi.org/10.1007/s00146-024-02087-8

112. Elena Ðerić, Domagoj Frank, Marin Milković (2025). Trust in Generative AI Tools: A Comparative Study of Higher Education Students, Teachers, and Researchers. https://doi.org/10.3390/info16070622

113. Michael Wessel, Martin Adam, Alexander Benlian et al. (2025). Generative AI and its Transformative Value for Digital Platforms. https://doi.org/10.1080/07421222.2025.2487315

114. Timothy R. McIntosh, Teo Sušnjak, Tong Liu et al. (2023). From Google Gemini to OpenAI Q* (Q-Star): A Survey of Reshaping the Generative Artificial Intelligence (AI) Research Landscape. https://doi.org/10.48550/arxiv.2312.10868

115. Ieva Mainardi (2024). Change management: artificial intelligence (AI) at the service of public administrations. https://doi.org/10.1007/s00146-024-02136-2

116. Giovanna Culot, Matteo Podrecca, Guido Nassimbeni (2024). Artificial intelligence in supply chain management: A systematic literature review of empirical studies and research directions. https://doi.org/10.1016/j.compind.2024.104132

117. Linda D. Hollebeek, Choukri Menidjel, Marko Sarstedt et al. (2024). Engaging consumers through artificially intelligent technologies: Systematic review, conceptual model, and further research. https://doi.org/10.1002/mar.21957

118. Peter Adebowale Olujimi, Pius Adewale Owolawi, Refilwe Constance Mogase et al. (2025). Agentic AI Frameworks in SMMEs: A Systematic Literature Review of Ecosystemic Interconnected Agents. https://doi.org/10.3390/ai6060123

119. Bartosz Wilczek, Mario Haim, Neil Thurman (2024). Transforming the value chain of local journalism with artificial intelligence. https://doi.org/10.1002/aaai.12174

Conclusion

What follows from this point is less a question of whether generative intelligence will matter than how deeply it will be woven into ordinary decisions. The pattern that has emerged across work, education, business, and daily life is not one of a single system replacing a single role. It is a steady redistribution of effort. Some work becomes faster. Some becomes cheaper. Some becomes more accessible to people who previously lacked time, support, or expertise. And some becomes more exposed, because the parts that can be standardized are now easier to automate or imitate.

That redistribution is already visible in the places where language, planning, and coordination matter most. A growing share of knowledge work is built from pieces that can be drafted, summarized, translated, compared, or reorganized. Research on labor-market exposure suggests that many occupations contain at least some tasks that can be meaningfully assisted or altered by large language models, especially when those models are embedded in software rather than used in isolation [47]. That does not mean whole jobs vanish at once. It means the shape of work changes from the inside out, often beginning with the first draft, the first pass, or the first answer.

The same pattern appears in organizations. The companies and institutions that benefit most are usually not the ones that simply buy access to a model and leave existing processes untouched. They are the ones that rethink how work moves, where humans should intervene, and which decisions deserve extra scrutiny. That is why adoption is rarely just a technical matter. It is a question of design, governance, and trust. The tool itself may be easy to access, but integrating it responsibly requires clarity about purpose, risk, and accountability. Studies of adoption in software engineering, for example, show that individual habits, team norms, and the surrounding work environment all shape whether generative tools become a real capability or just another convenience layered onto old routines [32].

The broader economic effect will not be evenly distributed. Some sectors will feel pressure sooner because they depend heavily on text, analysis, customer interaction, documentation, or other cognitively intensive work. Others will change more slowly, not because they are immune, but because their bottlenecks lie elsewhere. Even within the same field, the impact will differ by task, by level of responsibility, and by how much of the work can be evaluated by clear rules. That unevenness is part of what makes the AI explosion hard to read in the moment. It does not arrive as a single visible break. It arrives as a series of small reassignments of effort, many of them easy to overlook until they accumulate.

That accumulation matters because the systems are not static. They improve through use, through competition, and through the feedback loops created when more people depend on them. The result is a moving target rather than a finished product. A tool that feels experimental today may be routine tomorrow, and a use case that seems harmless in one setting may become consequential in another. The practical challenge is not to predict every turn in advance. It is to recognize that the center of gravity has shifted. Generative intelligence is no longer something outside ordinary work and life. It is becoming part of the environment in which decisions are made.

This is why judgment remains the most valuable human capacity in the system. The machine can accelerate production, but it cannot decide what deserves attention, what tradeoff is acceptable, or what consequence matters most. It can help people move faster through a task, but speed alone does not create wisdom. In fact, speed can make bad choices easier to repeat. The more fluent the tool becomes, the more important it is to slow down at the points where verification, context, and responsibility matter. The human role is not disappearing; it is being concentrated where meaning, oversight, and consequence meet.

At the same time, the opportunity is real. Generative systems can lower barriers to entry, reduce drudgery, expand access to help, and give more people a way to turn rough intention into usable output. They can make it easier to learn, easier to communicate, easier to prototype, and easier to keep pace with work that would otherwise be overwhelming. The question is not whether those benefits exist. It is who learns to use them well, who builds them into durable habits, and who remains dependent on systems they do not understand.

The next stage of the AI explosion will be defined less by novelty than by normalization. The tools will become less dramatic and more embedded. They will show up inside familiar applications, common workflows, and everyday expectations. That makes adaptation more important, not less. People and institutions that treat this as a passing wave will likely be forced to catch up later, under worse conditions. Those that treat it as a structural change can begin making better choices now: where to delegate, where to verify, where to redesign, and where to preserve human discretion.

The future that emerges from that process will not be determined by technology alone. It will be shaped by habits, incentives, rules, and the willingness to keep asking a simple question: what should a machine do here, and what should remain human?

Appendix: A Practical AI Readiness Guide

Before AI becomes part of a routine, it has to be treated as a decision, not a default. That means pausing long enough to ask what problem is actually being solved, who will touch the output, and what changes if the system is wrong, incomplete, or simply not worth the effort. The organizations and individuals that do this well tend to move through a similar sequence: they clarify the use case, test the fit, set boundaries, and then decide whether the tool deserves a place in the workflow at all.

AI readiness checklist for individuals and teams

Readiness starts with deciding where AI belongs in the work, not with buying a tool and hoping it finds a use. For individuals, that means identifying the tasks that are frequent, text-heavy, repetitive, or mentally draining in a predictable way. Those are the places where generative systems tend to help first. For teams, it means mapping the workflow and marking the handoffs: who drafts, who reviews, who approves, who needs the result, and where delays or errors usually appear. If the process is already unclear, AI will not fix that confusion. It will usually make it move faster, which can be useful or dangerous depending on the task.

A simple way to test readiness is to ask how much the work depends on judgment versus production. If the main bottleneck is generating a first pass, organizing information, or turning rough material into something usable, AI may be a good fit. If the main bottleneck is accountability, trust, or high-stakes interpretation, the system should stay farther from the final decision. In practice, many jobs contain both kinds of work. A manager may use AI to summarize meeting notes, but not to decide how to handle a personnel issue. A marketer may use it to draft options, but not to approve claims. The key is to place the tool where speed helps and to keep human review where consequences matter.

Individuals should also check their own habits before they check the software. If a task already gets rushed, AI can amplify that tendency by making it easier to produce something that looks finished before it is fully thought through. Readiness therefore includes a discipline of verification: reading the output, checking names, dates, figures, and claims, and asking whether the result actually answers the original question. It also means noticing where the tool changes your thinking. If you start accepting the first answer because it is convenient, the software is no longer just assisting your work; it is shaping your standards.

For teams, readiness depends on shared rules, not just individual skill. People need to know what can be entered into a system, what cannot, and who is responsible for reviewing the output before it leaves the team. That matters because AI use often spreads informally before policy catches up. One person uses it for drafting, another for analysis, and a third for customer communication, all under different assumptions about privacy and quality. Clear boundaries reduce confusion and help teams avoid the common pattern in which a useful tool becomes a hidden risk. Public-sector and organizational change research has repeatedly shown that adopting AI is as much a management and responsibility challenge as it is a technical one [115].

The next question is whether the team has a good place to start. Readiness does not require an ambitious transformation. It requires one or two low-risk use cases where the value is easy to observe and the downside is manageable. Good starting points include summarizing internal documents, drafting routine correspondence, organizing research notes, or generating first-pass outlines. Bad starting points are the ones where the output would directly determine a legal, medical, financial, or reputational outcome without expert review. A team that begins with modest tasks can learn how the system behaves before it is allowed anywhere near more sensitive work.

It is also worth checking whether the organization has the supporting habits that AI adoption needs. Tools work better when the underlying process is already documented, the data is reasonably clean, and the output has a clear owner. They work worse when everyone expects the model to compensate for missing context or vague instructions. In that sense, readiness is partly operational hygiene. A team with a messy workflow may still benefit from AI, but only if it is willing to redesign the workflow instead of simply layering a chatbot on top of confusion. The more autonomous the system becomes, the more important it is to define where it can act and where it must stop [118].

A practical checklist for both individuals and teams can be kept short. Before using AI on a task, ask: Is the task repetitive enough to benefit from speed? Is the output low enough risk to review rather than trust? Do we know what data is being shared? Do we have a human responsible for the final result? Can we tell whether the tool is saving time or just creating more polished work that still needs the same amount of correction? If the answers are unclear, the work is not ready yet. If the answers are clear, the system can be introduced in a way that improves performance without quietly eroding judgment.

Questions to ask before adopting a new AI tool

Before adopting a new AI tool, the first question is not whether it looks impressive, but whether it solves a real problem that matters enough to justify the change. Many tools win attention by producing a striking demo: a polished draft, a quick summary, a slick interface, a voice that sounds confident. That can be useful, but it is not the same as fit. A better test is to ask what specific task will be improved, how often that task occurs, and what the current cost of doing it the old way actually is. If the answer is vague—"we should probably be using AI somewhere"—the tool is likely being pulled in by novelty rather than need.

The next question is where the tool sits in the workflow. A tool that helps at the edge of a process, such as drafting a message or summarizing notes, is very different from one that influences decisions, approvals, customer interactions, or records that others will rely on later. The closer the tool gets to final output, the more important it becomes to define who reviews it, what counts as acceptable quality, and where human judgment must remain in charge. In organizational settings, adoption succeeds more often when the workflow is redesigned around the tool instead of merely layering the tool on top of old habits [3]. If people are still doing the same handoffs, duplicating the same checks, and correcting the same bottlenecks, the AI may save a little time without changing much else.

It is also worth asking what the tool is actually trained or configured to do. Some systems are broad and flexible; others are narrow and more dependable within a smaller domain. A general-purpose assistant may be able to draft, summarize, translate, or brainstorm, but it may also require more supervision because it is trying to be useful across many contexts. A specialized tool may be less flashy, but more stable for a specific job. The question is not which category sounds more advanced. It is which one matches the task, the risk level, and the degree of precision you need.

Generative systems are often strongest when producing a first pass, a range of options, or a compressed version of something larger [1]. That is valuable, but it is not the same as guaranteed correctness.

Another essential question is what happens when the tool is wrong. Every AI system will fail sometimes; the practical issue is whether the failure is harmless, annoying, costly, or dangerous. If a mistake only means a draft needs revision, the risk is low. If a mistake could affect a customer, a student, a financial decision, a legal record, or a public statement, the bar is much higher. Before adoption, ask whether the output can be independently checked, whether the source material is reliable, and whether there is a clear fallback if the system produces something misleading. This matters because generative systems can sound more certain than they are, which makes weak output harder to spot quickly.

Privacy and data handling deserve the same level of scrutiny. Ask what information the tool will see, where that information goes, who can access it, and whether it is retained for training, logging, or vendor analysis. A tool may be convenient precisely because it accepts sensitive material with little friction, but that convenience can create hidden exposure. The safest approach is to treat input data as if it might be stored, reviewed, or exposed beyond the immediate interaction unless the vendor has made the protections and limits unmistakably clear. For many organizations, the most important adoption question is not "Can it do the task?" but "Can it do the task without creating a new security or compliance problem?" Security researchers have long warned that AI can be misused for deception, impersonation, and other harmful purposes, which is another reason to be careful about what a system is allowed to ingest and generate [6].

Cost should be assessed broadly, not just as a subscription fee. A tool that looks inexpensive can still be expensive if it creates review burden, training time, workflow disruption, or confusion about responsibility. Ask who will maintain it, who will monitor quality, who will answer questions when it fails, and who will decide whether it should be retired. Also ask whether the tool becomes more useful as more people use it, or whether it creates a new dependency on a vendor whose pricing, policies, or product direction could change. In practice, the real cost of adoption often shows up in coordination, not licensing.

Finally, ask whether the tool improves judgment or quietly replaces it. The best AI tools do not just produce output; they help people think more clearly, move faster, or compare options more effectively. The weaker ones invite overtrust by making the answer look finished before the work is actually done. That distinction matters in every setting, but especially where the output will be used by other people. A useful adoption rule is simple: if the tool cannot be explained, reviewed, and corrected by the people responsible for the result, it is not ready to sit inside the core of the workflow. The goal is not to avoid AI. The goal is to make sure the tool earns its place by reducing friction without reducing accountability.

A simple framework for evaluating risk and value

A simple way to judge an AI use case is to ask two questions at once: How much value could this create? and How much risk does it introduce? The first question is about upside. The second is about exposure. A tool can be exciting and still be a bad fit if the stakes are too high. It can also look modest and still be worth adopting if it removes a persistent bottleneck. The point is not to make the decision feel mathematical. The point is to avoid being dazzled by capability while ignoring consequence. Value usually comes from one of four places: speed, scale, quality, or access. Speed means the work gets done faster. Scale means the same effort reaches more people or covers more tasks. Quality means the output becomes more consistent, more complete, or easier to refine. Access means something that was previously expensive, slow, or unavailable becomes usable by more people. These benefits often overlap. A support team that uses AI to draft replies may save time, handle more cases, and give customers faster service. A student who uses AI to explain a concept may understand it more quickly and keep moving instead of getting stuck. The question is not whether the tool is impressive in the abstract. The question is whether it improves one of these four dimensions in a real workflow.

Risk is easier to miss because it is often hidden in the cost of being wrong. Some tasks can tolerate a rough first pass. Others cannot. A marketing draft, a meeting summary, or a brainstorming session may absorb mistakes with little harm, because a human can review and revise the result before it matters. A legal filing, a medical recommendation, a financial decision, or a public statement faces a different standard. In those settings, a plausible error can be more dangerous than an obvious one because it may pass through review unnoticed. The higher the cost of failure, the more carefully the tool has to be constrained. Generative systems are useful precisely because they produce fluent output quickly; that same fluency can make errors feel safer than they are.

One practical test is to ask where the system sits in the chain of responsibility. If AI is helping with a first draft that a person will inspect, the risk is usually lower than if it is making a recommendation that people may accept automatically. If the tool touches the final decision, the risk rises. If it affects customers, students, patients, or the public, the risk rises again. This is why the same model can be appropriate in one context and inappropriate in another. The issue is not the model alone. It is the combination of output, oversight, and consequence. Research on AI adoption in applied settings shows that individual, technological, and social factors all shape whether a tool is actually used well [32].

Another useful filter is to ask whether the task is reversible. Some AI uses are easy to undo. If a draft email is awkward, it can be rewritten. If a summary misses a point, it can be corrected. But some errors are costly to unwind. A mistaken instruction sent to a customer, a flawed analysis embedded in a report, or a bad decision made at scale can create downstream work that is far more expensive than the original task. Reversibility matters because it changes the acceptable level of experimentation. The more reversible the task, the more room there is to learn by doing. The less reversible it is, the more the system should be boxed in by review, logging, and clear human approval.

It also helps to separate visible value from hidden cost. Visible value is easy to see: shorter turnaround time, cleaner drafts, fewer repetitive steps. Hidden cost shows up later: more time spent checking output, new confusion about who is accountable, overreliance on a tool that weakens judgment, or a false sense of confidence in polished but incomplete work. A use case that looks efficient on paper can become expensive if it creates extra review work or lowers the quality of decisions. That is why a pilot should measure not only output speed, but also correction time, error rate, and the burden placed on the people who have to clean up after the system.

A simple decision rule can help. Favor AI when the task is frequent, text-heavy, repetitive, and low stakes; when a human can review the result; and when the upside is clear in one of the four value categories. Be cautious when the task is rare, high stakes, hard to reverse, or likely to be accepted without scrutiny. In the middle ground, test small. Use the tool on a narrow slice of work, define what success looks like, and keep a person responsible for the final call. The goal is not to prove that AI is always safe or always useful. The goal is to match the level of trust to the level of consequence.

That framing is especially important because generative AI is often adopted first where it feels easiest, not where it is most valuable. Convenience pulls people toward whatever is immediately available. But the better question is whether the tool earns its place in the workflow. If it creates real value without pushing risk beyond what the organization can manage, it belongs. If it saves time but erodes judgment, increases exposure, or blurs accountability, it needs tighter limits. The right use of AI is not the one that looks most advanced. It is the one that gives you more capability without quietly taking away control.

Suggested next steps for continued learning

The first step is to get specific about where generative AI can actually help you, because "learning more about AI" is too broad to guide action. For most readers, the useful questions are not abstract ones about whether the technology is transformative. They are narrower: Which parts of my work depend on drafting, sorting, summarizing, comparing, or explaining? Which parts are repetitive enough that a machine can save time without changing the meaning of the work? Which parts are sensitive enough that a machine should not touch them at all? The more concrete the question, the clearer the answer becomes.

It also helps to distinguish between using AI as a convenience and using it as a decision aid. A convenience tool removes friction. It helps you get from rough idea to usable draft, from long document to short summary, from scattered notes to organized outline. A decision aid does something more delicate: it helps you think through options, test assumptions, or surface blind spots. Those uses are more valuable, but they also require more discipline. When people rely on AI for judgment-heavy work without a review process, the tool can make weak thinking look polished. When they use it to expand their options before deciding, it can sharpen the work instead of replacing it.

That distinction is one reason the strongest users of generative AI tend to be the ones who already have a clear sense of purpose. They do not ask the system to "help with everything." They ask it to help with a defined task, in a defined context, with a defined standard for success. A manager may use it to prepare a first draft of a meeting brief, then compare the result against internal priorities. A student may use it to generate alternate explanations of a concept, then check which version actually clarifies the material. A professional may use it to turn rough notes into a clean outline, then revise the structure before sharing it. The machine contributes speed; the human contributes direction.

If you want to go deeper, one of the best habits is to study examples of AI use in settings that resemble your own. The point is not to copy a tool blindly, but to notice patterns: where people are saving time, where they are introducing mistakes, where the workflow changes more than expected, and where the tool is being used as a substitute for thought instead of a support for it. Research on collaborative decision-making suggests that the value of generative AI often comes from the interaction between human judgment and machine output, not from either one alone [49]. That is a useful lens because it shifts attention away from novelty and toward process.

For readers in business or leadership roles, it is worth looking beyond product demos and into workflow design. Case-based research on entrepreneurs and firms suggests that AI assistance can improve performance, but not evenly and not automatically [14]. The gains depend on the kind of problem being solved and on whether the tool is matched to the task. Open-ended work, ambiguous goals, and high-stakes decisions still require human framing. That means continued learning should include not just "what can the model do?" but "what kind of work am I trying to improve, and what does improvement actually mean here?"

Another useful area for continued learning is the risk side. As AI becomes easier to use, it also becomes easier to misuse, whether through impersonation, deception, automated spam, or the rapid production of misleading content. Security-oriented work has long emphasized that the same capabilities that make AI useful can also lower the cost of harmful behavior [6]. You do not need to become an expert in adversarial threats to benefit from that insight. You only need to develop the habit of asking what could go wrong if a tool is wrong, manipulated, or used by the wrong person.

Beyond that, the best learning path is often hands-on and incremental. Try one tool, one task, one review habit. Compare the machine's output with your own. Notice where it saves time, where it introduces cleanup work, and where it simply does not fit. Over time, that practical testing teaches more than a long list of features ever will. It also builds judgment, which is the real skill that carries across tools. The goal is not to become dependent on any one system. It is to become more fluent in deciding when AI is worth trusting, when it is worth checking, and when it is worth setting aside.

www.ingramcontent.com/pod-product-compliance
Lightning Source LLC
LaVergne TN
LVHW100319210926
848480LV00003B/1185
9781923817944